Collins

11+ English

Practice Papers
Book 3

Shelley Welsh

Introduction

The 11+ tests

In most cases, the 11+ selection tests are set by GL Assessment, CEM or the individual school. You should be able to find out which tests your child will be taking on the website of the school they are applying to or from the local authority.

These single subject practice test papers are designed to reflect the style of GL Assessment tests, but provide useful practice and preparation for all 11+ tests and common entrance exams.

The score achieved on these test papers is no guarantee that your child will achieve a score of the same standard on the formal tests. Other factors, such as the standard of responses from all pupils who took the test, will determine their success in the formal examination.

Collins also publishes practice test papers, in partnership with The 11 Plus Tutoring Academy, to support preparation for the CEM tests.

Contents

This book contains:

- four practice papers – Tests A, B, C and D
- a multiple-choice answer sheet for each test
- a complete set of answers, including explanations.

Further multiple-choice answer sheets can be downloaded from our website so that you can reuse these papers: collins.co.uk/11plus

English

English tests are used by schools to assess the ability of each child and determine whether they have attained the required standard of English skills, including reading comprehension, vocabulary, grammar, spelling and punctuation.

Getting ready for the tests

Spend some time talking with your child before they take the tests, so that they understand the purpose of the practice papers and how doing them will help them to prepare for the actual exam.

Agree with your child a good time to take the practice papers. This should be when they are fresh and alert. You also need to find a good place to work, a place that is comfortable and free from distractions. Being able to see a clock is helpful as they learn how to pace themselves.

Explain how they may find some parts easy and others more challenging, but that they need to have a go at every question. If they 'get stuck' on a question, they should just mark it with an asterisk and carry on. At the end of the paper, they may have time to go back and try again.

Multiple-choice tests

For this style of test, the answers are recorded on a separate answer sheet and not in the book. This answer sheet will be marked by a computer in the actual exam, so it is important that it is used correctly. Answers should be indicated by drawing a clear pencil line through the appropriate box and there should be no other marks. If your child indicates one answer and then wants to change their response, the first mark must be fully rubbed out. Practising with an answer sheet now will reduce the chance of your child getting anxious or confused during the actual test.

How much time should be given?

Allowing 50 minutes for each of these practice papers will give your child experience of the most likely test format. If your child has not finished after 50 minutes, ask them to draw a line to indicate where they are on the paper at that time, and allow them to finish. This allows them to practise every question type, as well as allowing you to get a score showing how many were correctly answered in the time available. It will also help you and your child to think about ways to increase speed of working if this is an area that your child finds difficult. If your child completes the paper in less than 50 minutes, encourage them to go through and check their answers carefully.

Marking

The answers are included at the back of the book. Award one mark for each correct answer. Half marks are not allowed. No marks are deducted for wrong answers.

Using the results

Look for trends in your child's performance – are there certain kinds of questions that they have difficulty with? If so, then discuss ways that they might address their performance in those areas. Offer feedback in a constructive, helpful way. For example, it may be that your child needs to read more fiction books and look up words that they don't know, in order to improve their vocabulary.

And finally...

Let your child know that tests are just one part of school life and that doing their best is what matters. Plan a fun incentive for after the 11+ tests, such as a day out.

Contents

Practice Test A 5

Practice Test B 17

Practice Test C 29

Practice Test D 41

Answers and Explanations 58

Practice Test A Answer Sheet 65

Practice Test B Answer Sheet 67

Practice Test C Answer Sheet 69

Practice Test D Answer Sheet 71

ACKNOWLEDGEMENTS

The author and publisher are grateful to the copyright holders for permission to use quoted materials and images.

Pages 6–7: From *The Secret Garden* by Frances Hodgson Burnett.
Pages 18–19: From *After* written by Pádraig Kenny and illustrated by Steve McCarthy. Text © 2025 Pádraig Kenny. Reproduced by permission of Walker Books Ltd, London, SE11 5HJ. www.walker.co.uk
Pages 30–31: From *Roman Boy* written by Tony Bradman. Copyright © 2024 Tony Bradman. Reproduced by permission of Walker Books Ltd, London, SE11 5HJ. www.walker.co.uk
Pages 49–50: 'Walking with Polar Bears' by James Draven, reprinted by permission, © James Draven

Every effort has been made to trace copyright holders and obtain their permission for the use of copyright material. The author and publisher will gladly receive information enabling them to rectify any error or omission in subsequent editions. All facts are correct at time of going to press.

Published by Collins
An imprint of HarperCollins*Publishers* Limited
1 London Bridge Street
London SE1 9GF

HarperCollins*Publishers*
Macken House, 39/40 Mayor Street Upper,
Dublin 1, D01 C9W8, Ireland

ISBN 9780008760618

First published 2026

10 9 8 7 6 5 4 3 2 1

© HarperCollins*Publishers* Limited 2026

All rights reserved. No part of this publication may be reproduced, stored in a retrieval system, or transmitted, in any form or by any means, electronic, mechanical, photocopying, recording or otherwise, without the prior permission of Collins.

Without limiting the exclusive rights of any author, contributor or the publisher of this publication, any unauthorised use of this publication to train generative artificial intelligence (AI) technologies is expressly prohibited. HarperCollins also exercise their rights under Article 4(3) of the Digital Single Market Directive 2019/790 and expressly reserve this publication from the text and data mining exception.

British Library Cataloguing in Publication Data.

A CIP record of this book is available from the British Library.

Author: Shelley Welsh
Publisher: Clare Souza
Commissioning Editor: Richard Toms
Project Management: Fiona Watson
Cover Design: Sarah Duxbury
Production: Bethany Brohm
Printed in India by Multivista Global Pvt. Ltd.

This book contains FSC™ certified paper and other controlled sources to ensure responsible forest management.

For more information visit: www.harpercollins.co.uk/green

English
Multiple-Choice
Practice Test A

Read these instructions carefully.

1. You must not open or turn over this booklet until you are told to do so.

2. The booklet contains a passage for you to read and some questions for you to answer. You can refer to the passage to check your answers as many times as you want. You will then need to complete some spelling, punctuation and word selection exercises.

3. This is a multiple-choice test, so select your answer from the options on the answer sheet. Mark only **one** answer for each question.

4. Make sure you draw a line firmly through the rectangle next to your answer. If you make a mistake, rub it out as well as you can and mark your new answer.

5. Try to do as many questions as you can. If you find that you cannot do a question, do not waste time on it but simply go on to the next one. If you are stuck on a question, choose the answer that you think is best.

6. Do all rough working on a separate sheet of paper.

7. You have 50 minutes to complete the test.

Read this passage carefully, then answer the questions that follow.

The Secret Garden

After her parents die, Mary Lennox leaves her home in India to live with her uncle in Yorkshire.

Mistress Mary felt a little awkward as she went out of the room. Yorkshire people seemed strange, and Martha was always rather a puzzle to her. At first she had
5 disliked her very much, but now she did not. The skipping-rope was a wonderful thing. She counted and skipped, and skipped and counted, until her cheeks were quite red, and she was more interested than she had
10 ever been since she was born. The sun was shining and a little wind was blowing— not a rough wind, but one which came in delightful little gusts and brought a fresh scent of newly turned earth with it. She
15 skipped round the fountain garden, and up one walk and down another. She skipped at last into the kitchen-garden and saw Ben Weatherstaff digging and talking to his robin, which was hopping about him. She
20 skipped down the walk toward him and he lifted his head and looked at her with a curious expression. She had wondered if he would notice her. She wanted him to see her skip.

25 "Well!" he exclaimed. "Upon my word. P'raps tha' art a young 'un, after all, an' p'raps tha's got child's blood in thy veins instead of sour buttermilk. Tha's skipped red into thy cheeks as sure as my
30 name's Ben Weatherstaff. I wouldn't have believed tha' could do it."

"I never skipped before," Mary said. "I'm just beginning. I can only go up to twenty."

"Tha' keep on," said Ben. "Tha' shapes well
35 enough at it for a young 'un that's lived with heathen. Just see how he's watchin' thee," jerking his head toward the robin. "He followed after thee yesterday. He'll be at it again today. He'll be bound to find out
40 what th' skippin'-rope is. He's never seen one. Eh!" shaking his head at the bird, "tha' curiosity will be th' death of thee sometime if tha' doesn't look sharp."

Mary skipped round all the gardens and
45 round the orchard, resting every few minutes. At length she went to her own special walk and made up her mind to try if she could skip the whole length of it. It was a good long skip and she began slowly,
50 but before she had gone half-way down the path she was so hot and breathless that she was obliged to stop. She did not mind much, because she had already counted up to thirty. She stopped with a little laugh of
55 pleasure, and there, lo and behold, was the robin swaying on a long branch of ivy. He had followed her and he greeted her with a chirp. As Mary had skipped toward him she felt something heavy in her pocket strike
60 against her at each jump, and when she saw the robin she laughed again.

"You showed me where the key was yesterday," she said. "You ought to show me the door today; but I don't believe you
65 know!"

THE SECRET GARDEN

The robin flew from his swinging spray of ivy on to the top of the wall and he opened his beak and sang a loud, lovely trill, merely to show off. Nothing in the world is quite as adorably lovely as a robin when he shows off—and they are nearly always doing it.

Mary Lennox had heard a great deal about Magic in her Ayah's stories, and she always said that what happened almost at that moment was Magic.

One of the nice little gusts of wind rushed down the walk, and it was a stronger one than the rest. It was strong enough to wave the branches of the trees, and it was more than strong enough to sway the trailing sprays of untrimmed ivy hanging from the wall. Mary had stepped close to the robin, and suddenly the gust of wind swung aside some loose ivy trails, and more suddenly still she jumped toward it and caught it in her hand. This she did because she had seen something under it—a round knob which had been covered by the leaves hanging over it. It was the knob of a door.

She put her hands under the leaves and began to pull and push them aside. Thick as the ivy hung, it nearly all was a loose and swinging curtain, though some had crept over wood and iron. Mary's heart began to thump and her hands to shake a little in her delight and excitement. The robin kept singing and twittering away and tilting his head on one side, as if he were as excited as she was. What was this under her hands which was square and made of iron and which her fingers found a hole in?

It was the lock of the door which had been closed ten years and she put her hand in her pocket, drew out the key and found it fitted the keyhole. She put the key in and turned it. It took two hands to do it, but it did turn.

And then she took a long breath and looked behind her up the long walk to see if any one was coming. No one was coming. No one ever did come, it seemed, and she took another long breath, because she could not help it, and she held back the swinging curtain of ivy and pushed back the door which opened slowly—slowly.

Then she slipped through it, and shut it behind her, and stood with her back against it, looking about her and breathing quite fast with excitement, and wonder, and delight.

She was standing inside the secret garden.

THE SECRET GARDEN

Now answer these questions, looking at the passage again if you need to. Choose the most suitable answer in each case. Mark it on your answer sheet.

1. '… she was more interested than she had ever been since she was born.' (lines 9–10)

    What does this sentence tell the reader about Mary?

    A Mary is only interested in skipping.

    B Mary felt her life hadn't been very exciting so far.

    C Mary had been a champion skipper in India.

    D Mary didn't enjoy skipping in India.

    E Mary isn't really interested in learning how to skip.

2. The words 'she skipped' are repeated in the first paragraph.

    What is the effect of this repetition?

    A It reminds us that Mary likes skipping.

    B It shows that Ben is constantly watching Mary.

    C It reflects the continuous action of Mary skipping.

    D It tells us that Mary is trying to get the robin's attention.

    E It shows that Mary is trying to make Martha jealous.

3. What suggests that Mary was proud of her skipping ability?

    A She hoped Martha was watching her skip.

    B She managed twenty skips without stopping.

    C She was very interested in skipping.

    D She knew the robin was impressed at her skipping.

    E She wanted Ben to see her skip.

4. How would you describe the weather on the day?

    A Wet and windy

    B Sunny with a gentle breeze

    C Cloudy and cold

    D Sunny with strong gales

    E Sunny but chilly

NOW GO ON TO THE NEXT PAGE

THE SECRET GARDEN

5. '… an' p'raps tha's got child's blood in thy veins instead of sour buttermilk.' (lines 27–28)

   What do Ben's words tell you about his opinion of Mary prior to seeing her skip?

   A Ben didn't feel that Mary belonged at the house.
   B Ben hadn't thought Mary would be any good at skipping.
   C Ben had thought Mary was annoying and childish.
   D Ben had been worried about Mary's health.
   E Ben hadn't formed a favourable impression of Mary.

6. 'He'll be bound to find out what th' skippin'-rope is.' (lines 39–40)

   What does Ben mean?

   A The robin will satisfy his curiosity about what a skipping-rope is.
   B The robin doesn't want to know about the skipping-rope.
   C The robin will find the skipping-rope if Mary loses it.
   D The robin is bound to know what a skipping-rope is.
   E The robin is disappointed in the skipping-rope.

7. Why didn't Mary mind that she had to stop her skipping?

   A She wanted to talk to the robin.
   B It gave her time to sit down and rest.
   C She wanted to explore the garden.
   D She had passed her previous record number of skips.
   E It gave her an opportunity to chat to Ben.

8. '… she felt something heavy in her pocket strike against her at each jump …' (lines 59–60)

   What was the heavy thing in Mary's pocket?

   A her diary
   B the skipping-rope
   C a key
   D a hammer
   E a door knob

NOW GO ON TO THE NEXT PAGE

THE SECRET GARDEN

9. How did Mary feel about the robin following her?
   A She was annoyed.
   B She was pleased.
   C She didn't care.
   D She was scared.
   E She was shy.

10. What is the narrator's opinion of robins?
    A They find robins annoying.
    B They think robins are vermin.
    C They think robins are too curious.
    D They think robins are beautiful singers.
    E They think robins destroy the plants.

11. 'Mary Lennox had heard a great deal about Magic in her Ayah's stories, and she always said that what happened almost at that moment was Magic.' (lines 72–75)

    What is the 'Magic' that Mary refers to?
    A The robin spoke to Mary.
    B There were fairies hiding in the garden.
    C Mary caught the robin in her hand.
    D The robin started singing a song.
    E A sudden gust of wind exposed a hidden door.

12. What do you think Ben Weatherstaff's occupation is?
    A lawyer
    B gardener
    C stable boy
    D butler
    E cook

13. What is the physical evidence that tells us that Mary is excited about finding the door?
    A She starts muttering frantically under her breath.
    B Her heart is thumping and her hands are shaking.
    C She takes a long breath and then another long breath.
    D She checks to see if anyone is coming.
    E She laughs when she sees the robin.

NOW GO ON TO THE NEXT PAGE

THE SECRET GARDEN

14. What did the square area of iron with the hole in it turn out to be?
    A   a metal grille
    B   a treasure chest
    C   a door key
    D   a door lock
    E   a bird table

15. Why do you think Mary had to use two hands to turn the key?
    A   The lock was stiff because it hadn't been opened for years.
    B   The key was huge and Mary had little hands.
    C   The door was overgrown with a curtain of ivy.
    D   She was scared she might drop the key.
    E   She wasn't sure whether to turn it clockwise or anti-clockwise.

16. Why does Mary look to see if anyone is coming?
    A   She's hoping Ben will come to help her open the door.
    B   She wants someone to take the robin away.
    C   She doesn't want to be seen going through the door.
    D   She wants to keep the door a secret from Martha.
    E   To check if Ben has seen her opening the door.

THE SECRET GARDEN

Now answer the following questions about the meanings of words as they are used in the passage.

17. What do the words 'tha" and 'thee' mean as used by Ben when he is making conversation with Mary from line 25?

    A   her

    B   you

    C   it

    D   me

    E   them

18. Which of these is closest in meaning to 'heathen'? (line 36)

    A   pagan

    B   natives

    C   inhabitants

    D   locals

    E   criminals

19. What does the phrase 'look sharp' mean as used in line 43?

    A   to avoid evil

    B   to resist temptation

    C   to regain control

    D   to smooth over

    E   to hurry up

20. Which of these is closest in meaning to 'chirp'? (line 58)

    A   hiccup

    B   nod

    C   twitter

    D   snarl

    E   yawn

THE SECRET GARDEN

Now answer the following questions about words and phrases from the passage.

21. 'Tha' shapes well enough at it for a young 'un that's lived with heathen.' (lines 34–36)
    What does Ben mean by 'Tha' shapes well enough at it'?
    A Your shape is good.
    B You're very fit.
    C You need to practise.
    D You're doing fine.
    E You look happy.

22. The narrator says the ivy 'had crept over wood and iron'. (lines 93–94)
    How is this quotation best described?
    A simile
    B rhetoric
    C alliteration
    D personification
    E metaphor

23. 'It was strong enough to wave the branches of the trees …' (lines 78–79)
    Which of these words is a pronoun?
    A It   B was   C to   D of   E the

24. 'Thick as the ivy hung, it nearly all was a loose and swinging curtain …' (lines 91–93)
    'a loose and swinging curtain' is an example of what literary technique?
    A simile
    B metaphor
    C alliteration
    D personification
    E rhetoric

25. 'What was this under her hands which was square and made of iron …?' (lines 99–100)
    Which of these words is a noun?
    A under
    B square
    C which
    D made
    E iron

NOW GO ON TO THE NEXT PAGE

SPELLING EXERCISE

In the following sentences, there are some spelling mistakes. On each numbered line you will see that there is either one mistake or no mistake. Find the group of words with the mistake in it and mark its letter on your answer sheet. If there is no mistake, mark the letter N.

26. Gabi couldn't believe the dammage caused by the storm in the middle of the night.
        A   B   C   D

27. We decided to stay elsewhere as the new hotel rates were rediculously high.
        A   B   C   D

28. The climbers arrived at the summat where they took in the amazing views.
        A   B   C   D

29. Our new furneture nicely complements the style of our Victorian cottage.
        A   B   C   D

30. When I eventually reached home, it was poring down and the road was flooded.
        A   B   C   D

31. Though undoubtedly sad to be retiring, our teacher ashored us she'd visit us.
        A   B   C   D

32. The shimmering diamonds were nestled in the velvet lining of the jewellery box.
        A   B   C   D

33. Our nieghbour's dog has been known to react quite viciously when he sees a cat.
        A   B   C   D

NOW GO ON TO THE NEXT PAGE

PUNCTUATION EXERCISE

In the following passage, there are some mistakes to do with punctuation and capital letters. In each numbered line, you will find either one mistake or no mistake. Find the group of words with the mistake in it and mark its letter on your answer sheet. If there is no mistake, mark the letter N.

No Time to Lose

34. If only sh'ed never made the decision to go looking for her lost watch!
    A   B   C   D

35. Gemma shook her head miserably as she clambered over the scratchy
    A   B   C   D

36. heather which lay like a purple blanket over the moorland 'There's no
    A   B   C   D

37. chance of me finding it in all that' she said to herself. 'It'd be like looking
    A   B   C   D

38. for a needle in a haystack. Before she knew it, the sky darkened and little
    A   B   C   D

39. drops of rain started to splatter on the spongy heather. Gemmas heart
    A   B   C   D

40. pounded as she realised she was going to be in double trouble she had
    A   B   C   D

41. lost her watch (a present from Dad! AND she was going to be late home, in the dark!
    A   B   C   D

NOW GO ON TO THE NEXT PAGE

WORD SELECTION EXERCISE

In the following passage, you have to pick the most appropriate word or group of words so that the passage makes sense. Choose one of the five answers on each line and mark its letter on your answer sheet.

Freddy Makes an Observation

42. The morning [flu A] [flown B] [flied C] [flew D] [flue E] by and soon it was time for lunch.

43. Freddy [sat A] [sitting B] [sits C] [were sitting D] [were sat E] next to Spike and, as expected,

44. Karl and his friends began to tease him [at A] [for B] [with C] [on D] [under E] sitting at the 'tough table'. Freddy noticed something

45. unusual about Karl's mouth when [they A] [them B] [he C] [she D] [I E] sneered. At first, he

46. thought it [can A] [might B] [ought to C] [should D] [wouldn't E] be his eyes playing tricks on him, but

47. when he looked [scared A] [again B] [before C] [tomorrow D] [earlier E], he clearly saw it: FANGS!

48. He couldn't take his [ears A] [hands B] [eyes C] [nose D] [friend E] off Karl's teeth. 'What are you looking at?' snarled Karl.

49. But when he realised Freddy was [stirring A] [storing B] [stalling C] [staying D] [staring E] at his mouth, he quickly closed it and sat down.

Freddy knew his eyes weren't deceiving him — there *was* something unusual going on.

END OF TEST

English
Multiple-Choice
Practice Test B

Read these instructions carefully.

1. You must not open or turn over this booklet until you are told to do so.

2. The booklet contains a passage for you to read and some questions for you to answer. You can refer to the passage to check your answers as many times as you want. You will then need to complete some spelling, punctuation and word selection exercises.

3. This is a multiple-choice test, so select your answer from the options on the answer sheet. Mark only **one** answer for each question.

4. Make sure you draw a line firmly through the rectangle next to your answer. If you make a mistake, rub it out as well as you can and mark your new answer.

5. Try to do as many questions as you can. If you find that you cannot do a question, do not waste time on it but simply go on to the next one. If you are stuck on a question, choose the answer that you think is best.

6. Do all rough working on a separate sheet of paper.

7. You have 50 minutes to complete the test.

After

After a technological collapse which has all but ended civilisation as we know it, Jen and her father try to build a new life.

"Tell me again how the world ended."

They were standing on a ridge overlooking the dead city. Even from this distance, Jen could see the roads gnarled and choked by rusted hulks of cars and trucks, and the gradual advance of decades-old vegetation. The sky was a dull grey, but just for a moment the sun shone through, and she saw the quick glint of orange on a window high up on a tall building.

A *skyscraper*. They were called that because they used to scrape the sky. That's what Father had told her.

Father had one foot on the lip of the ridge and was gripping his wooden staff. He scanned the horizon.

"I've told you before. Many times," he said.

"Tell me again."

He turned and looked at her, his forehead lined in curiosity. "Why?"

"Because it's a story and I like stories."

He picked up his backpack and shouldered it. It was only a small thing, but Jen always marvelled at how graceful he was, even when he did small things. And when he was still he was graceful also, which probably wouldn't make sense to anyone else, but it made sense to her. Still and graceful, like nothing she'd ever seen. The only thing she could compare him to was a series of pictures she'd once found in a book. They were pictures of a man dancing. He was wearing dark skin-tight clothes and in some pictures he was pirouetting through the air. In others he crouched, a look of fierce concentration on his face.

Father nodded. "Of course, how it ended. I suppose the world ended slowly at first, then gradually, then all at once."

Jen glared at him. "Tell me properly. That was the condensed version."

"It was, yes, but I told it well, don't you think?"

Jen rolled her eyes.

"You don't agree, Jen?"

Jen sighed as she picked up her own backpack. "Do you think there'll be food down there?"

"Most likely."

She tapped her forehead as a sign. Father nodded in understanding. His face relaxed and his worry lines disappeared.

"Excellent expression. It almost looks natural," said Jen.

"Do you think so?"

Father looked pleased, and Jen was even more impressed.

"First, people destroyed their own habitat and the habitat of other animals," said Father. "This was the slow method, a method so gradual that humanity as a whole didn't notice at first, and when they eventually did notice they chose to ignore it."

They were walking in the city now. The skyscrapers loomed over them as they passed beneath their vast cool shadows. They

AFTER

picked their way through the wreckage. Jen noticed the usual crazy zigzag pattern of the vehicles that clogged the road. Some were piled one on top of the other, their metal shells burst and buckled, doors hanging off, windows shattered.

"So, they just let it happen?" said Jen.

Father nodded. "Despite the protests of some."

"That makes no sense," said Jen.

"Humans make no sense," said Father.

Jen narrowed her eyes at him. "I make sense."

"Sometimes," said Father. He looked thoughtful for a moment, then he smiled. "That was a joke."

"I know."

"Was it good?"

Jen looked at him with mock pity.

Father smiled more broadly. "I shall make more."

"Make sure they're better than that one."

Jen spotted something on the ground. It was a soft toy, a pink and white animal. It looked like a rabbit. Thinking about rabbits made her stomach rumble. They hadn't caught any in a while. She liked rabbit. She picked up the toy and dusted it off. *This used to belong to someone*, she thought. *A child perhaps*. Thinking about it made her feel uneasy. Suddenly she didn't want to look at the wreckage any more. She put the rabbit in her backpack.

"And then?" she asked.

"The Singularity," said Father. "Mankind had evolved to a state where integration with machine systems became an accepted part of life. This integration meant a melding of the mechanical with the biological. From birth, people had microchips implanted that allowed them to access a vast information and living system."

Jen nodded. "They called it the Hive."

Father stopped and looked at her. "You've heard all this before, Jen. Why do you need to hear it again?"

"You know me, I like stories."

"Why?"

"They help make sense of things."

"And this one does exactly that?" asked Father mildly.

No, Jen wanted to say. *No, it makes no sense at all, but maybe one day it will. Maybe one day after you've told it to me often enough, I'll begin to understand it, but for now I don't. I don't understand this story at all, but I know it terrifies me.*

"And then?" she said.

Father always seemed to hesitate a second before this part of the story.

"And then the Flood," he said matter-of-factly. "A cataclysmic short circuit of the Hive that destroyed all systems connected to it, both inorganic and organic."

"So, machines failed and people with microchips in their heads had their brains fried."

"In essence, yes."

"And what was left of humanity was sent back to the Dark Ages."

Father looked at her.

"I read about the Dark Ages in a book." She gestured around her. "This seems like the Dark Ages."

"One could say that, I suppose. You are very perceptive, Jen."

Jen tapped the side of her head. "Book learning."

"Indeed."

"Do you think there'll be a library?"

"It is a city, Jen. There is always a library. But food first."

And, right on cue, Jen's belly grumbled again.

NOW GO ON TO THE NEXT PAGE

AFTER

Now answer these questions, looking at the passage again if you need to. Choose the most suitable answer in each case. Mark it on your answer sheet.

1. What does Jen observe that suggests the city is 'dead'? (line 3)
    A The sky is a dull grey colour.
    B The sun shining through the clouds for a moment.
    C Discarded vehicles and decades-old vegetation.
    D A quick glint of orange in a window.
    E Lots of tall buildings called skyscrapers.

2. Why is Jen's father's forehead 'lined in curiosity'? (line 19)
    A He doesn't recognise her.
    B He's wondering why she wants to hear the same story again.
    C He has one foot on the lip of the ridge.
    D He is trying to work out where Jen is going.
    E He is very old and a bit bewildered.

3. What fills Jen with wonder about her father?
    A His small body
    B His gracefulness
    C His backpack
    D The small things he does
    E His stories

4. To what does Jen compare her father?
    A a magician
    B an elf
    C a wizard
    D a warrior
    E a dancer

NOW GO ON TO THE NEXT PAGE

AFTER

5. What movement does the man in the pictures make when he is not pirouetting?
   A He leaps
   B He nods
   C He is still
   D He crouches
   E He spins

6. Why does Jen say to her father, 'That was the condensed version.'? (line 39)
   A He doesn't tell the story in a way she can understand.
   B He tells her a shortened version of the end of the world.
   C They don't agree on how the world ended.
   D He is trying to protect her from the truth.
   E He is rushing to find food for them both.

7. Why does Jen sigh in line 43?
   A She is frustrated with her father.
   B She is very hungry.
   C Her backpack is heavy.
   D She wants to tell Father a story.
   E She's fed up that the world has ended.

8. Why did humanity not initially notice that they were destroying their habitat?
   A It happened too fast.
   B No one had any sense.
   C They had been brainwashed.
   D It happened so slowly.
   E They were being ignored.

AFTER

9. 'Humans make no sense,' said Father.

   Jen narrowed her eyes at him. 'I make sense.' (lines 72–73)

   Why does Jen narrow her eyes at her father?

   A She is angry with him for not telling her the full story.

   B She is letting him know she doesn't appreciate him saying 'Humans make no sense.'

   C She is struggling to see her father in the gloom.

   D It shows she doesn't really understand what he's saying.

   E It shows that she knows her father doesn't really know what he's saying.

10. Why does thinking about the toy rabbit make Jen 'feel uneasy'? (line 91)

    A It makes her think how hard it is to find food.

    B She feels guilty because she knows she's going to steal it.

    C It's a reminder that its owner may have died.

    D In case the rabbit's owner comes to look for it.

    E It's a reminder of the times when people had pets.

11. Why might Jen's father 'hesitate a second' (line 119) before telling the story of the Flood?

    A It is an upsetting part of the story, where humanity is virtually destroyed.

    B It is difficult for him to remember this part of the story.

    C It reminds him of Noah's Ark.

    D It makes him think of the Dark Ages.

    E It reminds him of when Jen was microchipped.

12. Jen says, 'And what was left of humanity was sent back to the Dark Ages.' (lines 129–130)

    Why does her father look at her after Jen says this?

    A He thinks she is making it up.

    B He doesn't know what the Dark Ages are.

    C He has bought her a book about the Dark Ages as a surprise.

    D He wonders if she is joking with him.

    E He is wondering where she's heard about the Dark Ages.

NOW GO ON TO THE NEXT PAGE

AFTER

13. What does Jen think might help her to understand the story of the end of the world?
    A   If she could read more about it in a library.
    B   If she could meet more survivors.
    C   If her father keeps retelling the story when she asks him to.
    D   If her father could remove her implanted microchip.
    E   If her father allowed her to get an education.

14. 'You are very perceptive, Jen.'
    Jen tapped the side of her head. (lines 135–137)
    Why does Jen tap the side of her head?
    A   To indicate to her father that she's heard that before.
    B   To indicate to her father that she has brains.
    C   To indicate to her father that she has a headache.
    D   To indicate to her father that she thinks he is mad.
    E   To indicate to her father that she has an implanted microchip.

NOW GO ON TO THE NEXT PAGE

AFTER

Now answer the following questions about the meanings of words as they are used in the passage.

15. Which word is closest in meaning to 'gnarled'? (line 4)
    A blocked
    B furrowed
    C knotted
    D flooded
    E churned

16. Which word is closest in meaning to 'pirouetting'? (line 32)
    A jumping
    B flying
    C climbing
    D falling
    E spinning

17. Which word is closest in meaning to 'In essence'? (line 128)
    A Unfortunately
    B Strangely
    C Mainly
    D Potentially
    E Basically

NOW GO ON TO THE NEXT PAGE

AFTER

Now answer the following questions about words and phrases from the passage.

18. 'This integration meant a melding of the mechanical with the biological.' (lines 98–99)

    What type of word is 'melding'?

    A adjective

    B pronoun

    C verb

    D noun

    E adverb

19. What type of words are the following? (lines 7–9)

    dull   quick   tall

    A adjectives

    B verbs

    C nouns

    D adverbs

    E prepositions

20. 'This seems like the Dark Ages.' (lines 133–134)

    How is this quotation best described?

    A a metaphor

    B a description

    C a phrase

    D a fact

    E a simile

SPELLING EXERCISE

In the following passage, there are some spelling mistakes. On each numbered line you will see that there is either one mistake or no mistake. Find the group of words with the mistake in it and mark its letter on your answer sheet. If there is no mistake, mark the letter N.

The Garden in Spring

21. | Vibrant clusters | of flowers bloom | along the edges | of the cobbelstone path. | As |
    | A | B | C | D | |

22. | your eye travels | to the far corner | of the lush green lawn, | you will catch a glimse of soft |
    | A | B | C | D |

23. | pink petals dancing | from the branches | of the narled | and twisted blossom tree. |
    | A | B | C | D |

24. | A collection | of chipped plant pots | showcases an abundance | of flowers: striking |
    | A | B | C | D |

25. | crocuses, | delicate daffodils | and dazzling red tulips. | Buzzing bees meander |
    | A | B | C | D |

26. | steadily around the garden, | visiting the | colourful blooms | to collect their golden |
    | A | B | C | D |

27. | tresures. | Bluebirds, red robins | and finches | busily nibble at the seeds on the |
    | A | B | C | D |

28. | wooden birdfeeder | which hangs lazely | from a huge | old oak tree while a |
    | A | B | C | D |

29. | marmelade cat | looks on and licks his lips, | luxuriating | in the warm sun. |
    | A | B | C | D |

30. | A sudden breeze | disturbs the grass | and the trees | shake there branches, |
    | A | B | C | D |

31. | sprinkling glittering | dropplets of dew | on the earth below. | The garden seems to |
    | A | B | C | D |

32. | yawn and stretch, | welcomeing the new dawn. | It is spring! | The rebirth has begun. |
    | A | B | C | D |

NOW GO ON TO THE NEXT PAGE

PUNCTUATION EXERCISE

In the following sentences, there are some mistakes to do with punctuation and capital letters. On each numbered line, you will find either one mistake or no mistake. Find the group of words with the mistake in it and mark its letter on your answer sheet. If there is no mistake, mark the letter N.

33. Vincent went to the shops to buy some: fruit apples, bananas, oranges and pears.
    | A | B | C | D |

34. When Flo realised she had missed, the goal she put her head in her hands and cried.
    | A | B | C | D |

35. Orla holds a hairbrush with her left hand but she is actually right-handed
    | A | B | C | D |

36. "I havent a clue how to assemble this," sighed Sam, looking at the pile of screws.
    | A | B | C | D |

37. We're having a sleepover at Mayas house for her birthday this time next week.
    | A | B | C | D |

38. Dublin, the capital city of ireland, is an exciting place to visit for a long weekend.
    | A | B | C | D |

39. Without further ado, Amy marched over to the bully and gave her a piece of her mind.
    | A | B | C | D |

40. "Is there any point in watching the match," asked Zac. "They're bound to lose!"
    | A | B | C | D |

41. "Theres no way I'm walking up that mountain," I wailed. "It's too steep!"
    | A | B | C | D |

42. We went cycling last weekend (our favourite activity and bumped into Martin.
    | A | B | C | D |

43. Next Summer, we are visiting my cousin in Denmark – we've not seen her for years.
    | A | B | C | D |

44. The dogs chased the ducks around the pond the park-keeper wasn't impressed.
    | A | B | C | D |

NOW GO ON TO THE NEXT PAGE

WORD SELECTION EXERCISE

In the following passage, you have to pick the most appropriate word or group of words so that the passage makes sense. Choose one of the five answers on each line and mark its letter on your answer sheet.

Jack and Rose Take a Stroll

45. Politely, Jack offered his [leg A] [arm B] [ear C] [knee D] [foot E] for Rose to link and they proceeded

46. to stroll down the deck. As they [took A] [take B] [have taken C] [was taking D] [had took E] in the fresh

47. evening air, they told each other a little [at A] [by B] [to C] [about D] [of E] themselves. Rose laughed

48. as Jack told her how he envied the comfort of First Class [when A] [as B] [while C] [therefore D] [for E]

49. Jack [has been A] [was B] [is C] [had been D] [were E] amazed to learn that the adventurous Rose had

50. peeked [by A] [above B] [at C] [through D] [for E] a window to watch with envy as Third Class enjoyed

51. a night of singing and dancing. Both knew it [could A] [wouldn't B] [shouldn't C] [oughtn't D] [can't E]

52. do to be seen together; the very thought of [which A] [that B] [when C] [who D] [what E] her mother

53. would say made Rose's stomach churn! As for Jack, he'd [undertake A] [give B] [try C] [get D] [getting E]

54. a clip round his ear [from A] [with B] [and C] [for D] [by E] his fellow passengers for having ideas above his

55. [station A] [mind B] [brain C] [feet D] [occupation E]. As the seas began to surge, Rose

56. held on more [slackly A] [weakly B] [lovely C] [promptly D] [firmly E] to Jack's arm.

END OF TEST

English
Multiple-Choice
Practice Test C

Read these instructions carefully.

1. You must not open or turn over this booklet until you are told to do so.

2. The booklet contains a passage for you to read and some questions for you to answer. You can refer to the passage to check your answers as many times as you want. You will then need to complete some spelling, punctuation and word selection exercises.

3. This is a multiple-choice test, so select your answer from the options on the answer sheet. Mark only **one** answer for each question.

4. Make sure you draw a line firmly through the rectangle next to your answer. If you make a mistake, rub it out as well as you can and mark your new answer.

5. Try to do as many questions as you can. If you find that you cannot do a question, do not waste time on it but simply go on to the next one. If you are stuck on a question, choose the answer that you think is best.

6. Do all rough working on a separate sheet of paper.

7. You have 50 minutes to complete the test.

Roman Boy

Read this passage carefully, then answer the questions that follow.

Roman Boy

Lucius lives with his mother and stepfather in a big house on the Esquiline Hill in Rome. The year is 125 CE.

... the winter before last, his father Drusus Caecina Placidus had died of a wasting sickness, and after the usual year of mourning, Lucius's mother had married again. So they had
5 come to live in the house of her new husband.

His name was Gaius Metellus Corbulo, and he was an important man, which meant he could afford a big house on the Esquiline Hill. Lucius's room, his *cubiculum*, was next
10 to the *atrium*, the entrance to the house, a space open to the sky with a pond in the middle. A display of wax faces covered one wall of the *atrium*, the death masks of Gaius's ancestors, and beside that was the shrine to
15 the household Gods, the *Lares* and *Penates*. Lucius went through the *atrium* and past the *tablinium*, the study where Gaius spoke to his many followers, the people who depended on him. Beyond that was the *triclinium*, the dining
20 room, its walls covered in pictures of the Gods.

Gaius was in none of those rooms, so Lucius made for the *peristylium*, the garden at the heart of the house. It was open to the sky like the *atrium*, but it was larger, with
25 a much bigger pond, and was filled with flowers and plants in terracotta pots.

On the far side was a wide terrace that looked down on the city below. Gaius was sitting there on a wooden bench, talking
30 quietly to Lucius's mother. It was the early evening of a late summer day that had been very hot, but high on the Esquiline Hill a cool breeze brought some relief. Lucius could hear a faint buzzing in the distance,
35 the city's constant background noise. As always, two slave girls stood in the shadows at the end of the terrace, waiting to do the bidding of their master and mistress.

Lucius stopped at a respectful distance.
40 "Please, sir ... may I speak with you about something?" he said, the words he had practised tumbling from his lips.

"Oh really, Lucius," his mother said crossly. "You mustn't bother Gaius."

45 Lucius glanced at her. She was wearing a gown of green silk, and her long dark hair was plaited and piled on her head in the fashionable style. There were gold rings on her fingers and a fine gold chain around
50 her slender neck. Like most Roman women, Lucius's mother had married young, becoming the wife of Lucius's father at the age of thirteen – he had been twenty-eight. She was thirty now, and still lovely, tall and slim with
55 pale skin and brown eyes. People said Lucius looked like his mother. He did have her eyes and dark hair, and was quite tall for his age.

Lucius often thought the marriage must have seemed a good match. Both husband
60 and wife were of old noble families, and Lucius's father was doing well in his career. But things had gone wrong. His father had turned out to be a drinker and gambler, and he had lost most of his money. There had
65 been bitter arguments, and Lucius knew his mother wasn't unhappy when his father died, mourning him only because it was expected. Lucius couldn't blame her. He hadn't been close to his father either.

70 "Peace, Cornelia," said Gaius. "Let the boy speak. It seems important."

ROMAN BOY

She lowered her eyes in obedience, and Lucius turned to his stepfather. Gaius was in his fifties, but he was fit and lean, his hair still mostly black. His nose was large and bony, his eyes hazel, his gaze watchful – Lucius sometimes thought he looked like a hawk. Gaius rarely smiled, and when he did there was no joy in it. He had spent the day at the Forum, talking to other important men, all wearing their white togas folded in the traditional way. Now he had changed into a blue tunic.

Lucius knew Gaius had married his mother for more than just her beauty. Gaius was ambitious, but his family was neither as old nor as noble as Cornelia's, and such things counted in Rome. Money was important, and Gaius had plenty – his family owned lots of land, and they had made a fortune in their business dealings as traders. Yet none of that was enough. If you wanted to reach the top in Rome, you had to be connected to one of the ancient families – by birth, or at least by marriage.

"It *is* important," said Lucius, looking into his eyes. "Well, it is for me, at least. I've been, er … wondering if … well, if I could … ask you to adopt me as your son."

Lucius saw his mother's eyes widen, but she said nothing. Gaius tipped his head to one side, studying him as a hawk might examine its prey before swooping.

"I see …" said Gaius. "You do realize that would involve certain … obligations on my part? Besides, I already have three living sons. Why do I need another?"

Gaius had been married twice before, and Lucius knew he had divorced his last wife so he could marry Cornelia. Gaius's sons were grown men, and as things stood, they would inherit his wealth. But if Lucius were adopted, he would have the rights of a son too. Till then he was little more than a lodger in his stepfather's house.

"Most people think a man can never have too many sons," said Lucius.

"And some people might think that far too clever an answer." Gaius slowly leaned forward, his hard eyes fastening on Lucius's. "Now let us be completely honest with each other, shall we, Lucius? Tell me, what is it that you *really* want?"

Lucius had been expecting Gaius to need some persuading, and he had prepared many things to say. But he hadn't expected Gaius to ask him that. Suddenly he sensed his whole life might hinge on this moment, on what he said next. He touched his *bulla** and sent a silent prayer to Jupiter – *Lord of the Sky, I beg you, help me choose the right words* – and then it was as if the God spoke through his mouth.

"I want to be like you," Lucius said, holding Gaius's gaze. "I want to be rich and powerful. I don't want a life like my father's, one that ends with nothing."

"A much better answer." Gaius gave him one of those rare, wintry smiles of his. "And of course you will need my help to make your way in the world."

"That is all I am asking of you, sir," said Lucius. "I have no other male relatives on either side of my family to set me on the right path. You are my only hope."

Such was the custom for the boys of Rome's noble families, as it always had been. In Rome, men held all the power – their wives and children had to obey. But both Lucius's grandfathers had long since died, and he had no living uncles, no older brothers who could give him advice or introductions to men who might help him. There were not even any male friends of the family. His father had seen to that.

"You should be proud of your boy, Cornelia," Gaius said at last. "It is good to see ambition in one so young. He reminds me of myself when I was his age."

* *A bulla is a gold locket chain that Roman boys were given at birth for luck and to protect them from evil spirits.*

ROMAN BOY

Now answer these questions, looking at the passage again if you need to. Choose the most suitable answer in each case. Mark it on your answer sheet.

1. Why was Lucius's stepfather able to live in a big house on the Esquiline Hill?
   A   He was the mayor of Rome.
   B   He was married to Lucius's mother.
   C   He had lots of ancestors.
   D   He was a rich, important man.
   E   He was a Roman god.

2. What is the Roman word for 'room'?
   A   *atrium*
   B   *cubiculum*
   C   *tablinium*
   D   *peristylium*
   E   *triclinium*

3. What does the household of Gaius Metellus Corbulo contain that suggests the Gods are worshipped?
   A   death masks
   B   terracotta pots
   C   wax faces
   D   a pond in the garden
   E   a shrine and pictures of the Gods

4. 'Lucius could hear a faint buzzing in the distance …' (lines 33–34)
   What does the 'faint buzzing' refer to?
   A   bees visiting the flowers
   B   the sound of Gaius chatting to Cornelia
   C   the two slave girls muttering
   D   the sound of activity in the city
   E   the nervous tremor from Lucius's lips

NOW GO ON TO THE NEXT PAGE

ROMAN BOY

5. 'As always, two slave girls stood in the shadows at the end of the terrace …' (lines 35–37)

   Why do you think the slave girls were standing in the shadows?

   A They were hiding from their master and mistress.

   B They felt shy when they saw Lucius.

   C They were sheltering from the cool breeze.

   D They were praying to their master and mistress.

   E They were staying out of sight until called for.

6. '"Please, sir … may I speak with you about something?" he said, the words he had practised tumbling from his lips.' (lines 40–42)

   What does the fact that Lucius 'had practised' the words tell the reader?

   A The words were difficult to pronounce.

   B He was concerned he might stutter.

   C He was anxious about approaching Gaius.

   D He didn't speak the Roman language fluently.

   E He didn't know the traditional way of approaching a nobleman.

7. Why was Lucius's mother not unhappy when his father had died?

   A His father had been cruel to her.

   B The marriage had never been a good match.

   C His father had not done well in his career.

   D His father had not come from an old noble family.

   E His father had lost most of his money.

ROMAN BOY

8. Why did Lucius's mother grieve for his father despite their bitter arguments?
    A   She loved him in spite of everything.
    B   A widow was expected to grieve.
    C   So that Lucius wouldn't be embarrassed.
    D   Women had to show obedience.
    E   To show that death was important.

9. What was more important than money to the Romans?
    A   a house on top of the Esquiline Hill
    B   a connection to ancient nobility
    C   showing that you worshipped the Gods
    D   marrying a beautiful young woman
    E   trading and owning lots of land

10. What is Gaius's initial reaction to Lucius's request?
    A   He reacts with furious indignation.
    B   He is proud that Lucius wants to be adopted.
    C   He reacts with calm consideration.
    D   He paces up and down the terrace.
    E   He widens his eyes in complete surprise.

11. Why does Lucius want Gaius to adopt him?
    A   He wants to have the same surname as his mother.
    B   He wants to be closer to his three stepbrothers.
    C   He wants to be a lodger in Gaius's house.
    D   He wants the same rights as his three stepbrothers.
    E   He thinks Gaius will benefit from having another son.

ROMAN BOY

12. Why did Lucius sense that '… his whole life might hinge on this moment, on what he said next'? (lines 127–129)

    A   He thought Gaius could be easily persuaded.

    B   The right response was essential if he were to get what he wanted.

    C   He knew Gaius had the potential to end his life.

    D   He sensed that Jupiter was speaking through his mouth.

    E   He sensed that Gaius was trying to trick him.

13. Why do you think Gaius gave Lucius 'one of those rare, wintry smiles of his'? (line 139)

    A   He was flattered by Lucius's response.

    B   He thought Lucius's response was hilarious.

    C   He was pleased that Lucius had held his gaze.

    D   He was pleased Lucius did not want a life like his father's.

    E   He thought it was funny that Lucius prayed to Jupiter.

14. Why was Gaius Lucius's 'only hope'? (line 145)

    A   It was the custom for boys in noble families to say that to their elders.

    B   Men held all the power and their wives and children had to obey.

    C   It was what Jupiter, to whom Lucius has sent a silent prayer, had told him.

    D   Lucius has tried asking Jupiter for help, but to no avail.

    E   Lucius has no other male relatives or male family friends with connections.

15. What is the narrator suggesting when he says 'His father had seen to that.'? (line 155)

    A   That Lucius's father had only wanted female family friends.

    B   That Lucius's father hadn't wanted advice from anyone.

    C   That Lucius's father had lost any male family friends.

    D   That Lucius's father was jealous of male family friends.

    E   That Lucius's father didn't want male friends courting his wife.

NOW GO ON TO THE NEXT PAGE

ROMAN BOY

Now answer the following questions about the meanings of words as they are used in the passage.

16. Which of these phrases is closest in meaning to 'to do the bidding of'? (lines 37–38)
    A   to carry out the wishes of
    B   to carry out the intentions of
    C   to attend to the serving of
    D   to do the cleaning of
    E   to carry out the fanning of

17. Which of these is closest in meaning to 'noble'? (line 60)
    A   religious
    B   wealthy
    C   intellectual
    D   royal
    E   aristocratic

18. Which English word is most closely related to the Roman word '*cubiculum*'? (line 9)
    A   cuboid
    B   cubicle
    C   cabin
    D   caravan
    E   cupboard

19. Which of these is closest in meaning to 'slender'? (line 50)
    A   gnarled
    B   long
    C   bony
    D   slim
    E   stout

20. 'His nose was large and bony, his eyes hazel, his gaze watchful …' (lines 75–76)
    Which of these is closest in meaning to 'hazel'?
    A   greenish-brown
    B   oval
    C   bluey-green
    D   round
    E   nutty

NOW GO ON TO THE NEXT PAGE

ROMAN BOY

Now answer the following questions about words and phrases from the passage.

21. Lucius's stepfather studied him 'as a hawk might examine its prey'. (lines 102–103)

    How is this phrase best described?

    A a description

    B a clause

    C a simile

    D a metaphor

    E a noun phrase

22. 'His nose was large and bony, his eyes hazel, his gaze watchful …' (lines 75–76)

    What type of word is 'watchful'?

    A an adjective

    B a verb

    C an adverb

    D a noun

    E a preposition

23. 'Suddenly he sensed his whole life might hinge on this moment …' (lines 127–128)

    Which of these words is a verb?

    A Suddenly   B whole   C life   D hinge   E moment

24. 'But if Lucius were adopted, he would have the rights of a son too.' (lines 112–114)

    What verb form is 'were adopted'?

    A simple past

    B past progressive

    C present progressive

    D past perfect

    E subjunctive

25. '… the winter before last, his father Drusus Caecina Placidus had died of a wasting sickness, and after the usual year of mourning, Lucius's mother had married again.' (lines 1–4)

    Which of these is an adverbial phrase?

    A the winter before last

    B his father

    C a wasting sickness

    D the usual year

    E had married

NOW GO ON TO THE NEXT PAGE

SPELLING EXERCISE

In the following sentences, there are some spelling mistakes. On each numbered line you will see that there is either one mistake or no mistake. Find the group of words with the mistake in it and mark its letter on your answer sheet. If there is no mistake, mark the letter N.

26. The journalists attended the press conference expecting an instant update on events.
    A — B — C — D

27. Giselle ate a harty breakfast of porridge, scrambled eggs and buttered toast.
    A — B — C — D

28. Ria bought a mixture of paints and stationary items from the craft shop.
    A — B — C — D

29. I expressed my sincere condolances to my neighbour on the loss of his pet tarantula.
    A — B — C — D

30. I was somewhat aggrieved to learn that the theatrical performance would not visit my town.
    A — B — C — D

31. Greg was overwhelmed with fatige and hunger after trekking for eight days.
    A — B — C — D

32. Dad always expects me to excel in tests so I occasionally exagerate my score.
    A — B — C — D

33. Ruth gestered towards the door, indicating that Jay should make himself scarce.
    A — B — C — D

NOW GO ON TO THE NEXT PAGE

PUNCTUATION EXERCISE

In the following passage, there are some mistakes to do with punctuation and capital letters. On each numbered line, you will find either one mistake or no mistake. Find the group of words with the mistake in it and mark its letter on your answer sheet. If there is no mistake, mark the letter N.

Football Fun

34. "We mustn't be late, Abbi," said Chloe pointing, dramatically at her watch.
          A   B   C   D

35. "Remember last time when we missed the first half?" she added "That was
          A   B   C   D

36. because you had hiccups and insisted on stopping for a bottle of water?"
         A   B   C   D

37. "you really do tell porkies," Abbi said. "We missed ten minutes at most."
         A   B   C   D

38. "Anyway, lets hope we win today. I think Tina is our best bet in goal."
         A   B   C   D

39. The girls made their way through the turnstile, skipped down the steps and took their seats.
          A   B   C   D

40. "I do enjoy our football get togethers," said Chloe. "Especially when we're on time."
         A   B   C   D

41. Their team won (the score was 3 – 0 so the pair celebrated with an ice-cream.
         A   B   C   D

NOW GO ON TO THE NEXT PAGE

WORD SELECTION EXERCISE

In the following passage, you have to pick the most appropriate word or group of words so that the passage makes sense. Choose one of the five answers on each line and mark its letter on your answer sheet.

Ciaran the Conqueror

42. Last Monday, our very own local | exercise (A) | expedition (B) | explorer (C) | exclusive (D) | exhibition (E) |

43. Ciaran Shaw conquered Kilimanjaro for the | frequent (A) | then (B) | one (C) | next (D) | first (E) | time.

44. Years of hard training | but (A) | and (B) | or (C) | with (D) | also (E) | dedication

45. | meant (A) | means (B) | mend (C) | meaned (D) | main (E) | that Ciaran was

46. finally able to | reach (A) | stand (B) | fall (C) | grow (D) | leave (E) | the summit.

47. | Despite of (A) | In spite (B) | Despite (C) | Spite of (D) | In despite (E) | the freezing

48. cold weather, Ciaran managed to | piece (A) | place (B) | post (C) | pinch (D) | plaice (E) |

49. his flag on the snowy | peek (A) | plaque (B) | plain (C) | peak (D) | plant (E) | and smile for the camera.

END OF TEST

English
Multiple-Choice Practice Test D

Read these instructions carefully.

1. You must not open or turn over this booklet until you are told to do so.

2. The booklet contains two passages for you to read and some questions for you to answer. You can refer to the passages to check your answers as many times as you want. You will then need to complete some spelling and word selection exercises.

3. This is a multiple-choice test, so select your answer from the options on the answer sheet. Mark only **one** answer for each question.

4. Make sure you draw a line firmly through the rectangle next to your answer. If you make a mistake, rub it out as well as you can and mark your new answer.

5. Try to do as many questions as you can. If you find that you cannot do a question, do not waste time on it but simply go on to the next one. If you are stuck on a question, choose the answer that you think is best.

6. Do all rough working on a separate sheet of paper.

7. You have 50 minutes to complete the test.

Henry VIII

Henry VIII was born at Greenwich on 28 June 1491, the second son of Henry VII and Elizabeth of York. He became the heir to the throne in 1502 following the death of his
5 elder brother, Prince Arthur, and succeeded to the throne in 1509 after the death of his father.

In his youth, Henry would spend his days hunting (he could tire up to ten horses in
10 a day) and jousting. He was known for his lavish parties, spending large sums of money on food, drink and entertainment. Henry also enjoyed playing tennis and had courts built in his many palaces.

15 As well as his sporting prowess, he was also highly intelligent. He spoke good French, Latin and Spanish, was skilled in playing many musical instruments and was an accomplished composer.

20 Henry was a committed Roman Catholic and regularly attended mass. In 1521, he authored a best-selling book that attacked Martin Luther, a German Protestant priest who had criticised the Catholic Church.
25 As a reward for his staunch defence of the Catholic Church, the Pope gave Henry the title of Defender of the Faith.

When Henry acceded to the throne, the monarchy's finances were in a healthy state.
30 However, his lack of interest in government business meant he came to rely heavily on the advice of Thomas Wolsey.

The son of an Ipswich butcher, Wolsey was a successful priest and the personal chaplain
35 to Henry's father. His career continued to flourish under Henry VIII and he became Lord Chancellor in 1515. From 1515 to 1529, Wolsey's power was undisputed and he became one of the most influential
40 ministers in British history (he was often described as 'the other king'). He used his power and wealth to indulge his passion for building, symbolised by his construction of Hampton Court Palace which was larger
45 than anything the king possessed.

One of Henry's main achievements during his reign was the expansion of the Navy. While this was primarily to defend England from potential invasion by France and
50 Scotland, Henry was also motivated by the desire to show how much power England had and to assert English dominance on the seas. He invested significantly in the Navy, increasing its size from five ships to fifty-
55 three. One of these was the *Mary Rose*, the remains of which can be seen in the Portsmouth Naval Museum.

Henry had married his brother's widow, Catherine of Aragon, in 1509. Catherine
60 gave birth to six children but only one survived, a girl named Mary, born in 1516. By the late 1520s, Catherine was in her forties and Henry was desperate for a male heir. England had never had a ruling queen
65 and it was believed there was considerable risk associated with handing the Crown to a woman. People feared it could lead to a dispute about succession or to the domination of England by a foreign power
70 through marriage.

Having fallen in love with Anne Boleyn, and wanting a son, Henry tried to persuade the Pope to annul* his marriage on the grounds that it had never been legal because
75 Catherine had been married to his brother. (He was unable to divorce her as divorce was not legal in the Catholic Church at the time.)

HENRY VIII

When Henry's efforts failed, Wolsey stepped in but he too could not get the Pope to agree to annul the marriage. Already unpopular with those close to Anne, this failure saw Wolsey replaced as Lord Chancellor by Thomas Cromwell, who used the power of Parliament to resolve the problem by proposing a law that would transfer the authority to grant an annulment from the Pope to Henry himself. The Pope's influence in England was now diminished, eventually leading to the English Reformation when England broke away from the Catholic Church.

In 1532, Thomas Cranmer was promoted to Archbishop of Canterbury, and in May 1533 he declared Henry's marriage invalid. Anne Boleyn was crowned queen a week later.

As a result of this rejection of Catholic doctrine, Henry was excommunicated** by the Pope. This led to the passing of the Act of Supremacy in 1534 which established the Church of England, with the monarch as its head. The English Church had become independent from the Pope. Of course, many people opposed this and not long after the Act of Supremacy, Henry passed the Treasons Act which meant that anyone who questioned his power over the Church, or spoke ill of him, could be punished by death.

As Henry sought to consolidate both his royal and religious authority, he was supported by his Lord Chancellor, Thomas Cromwell, who had earlier decided that the monks, nuns and friars who resided in the country's many monasteries were corrupt, living in wealth and luxury unbecoming to their religious calling. He now sent men to confiscate their treasures and close the monasteries down, selling them and their land to the gentry. This was called the Dissolution of the Monasteries and was another step forward in Henry's intent to extinguish the power of the Catholic Church. The profits went to the king, who became exceedingly wealthy. Those monasteries that were not destroyed were taken over by noblemen who turned them into grand residences.

Anne did not produce Henry's much-longed-for son. She gave birth to a girl who would later be crowned Queen Elizabeth I. Henry accused Anne of treason and she was executed in 1536. Eventually, in 1537, Henry had a son, Edward, by his third wife, Jane Seymour, but she died twelve days later.

Henry made three more marriages: Anne of Cleves (they divorced), Katherine Howard (she was beheaded) and Catherine Parr (who survived Henry).

Henry died in 1547 and was succeeded by his son, Edward. Although often thought of only in terms of his many marriages, Henry should also be remembered for helping to create a more stable and centralised government, his investment in the country's Navy, his religious reforms which resulted in England becoming a Protestant nation and his patronage of the arts and education.

To declare a marriage to have had no legal existence.

**Excluded from the Roman Catholic Church.*

HENRY VIII

Now answer these questions, looking at the passage again if you need to. Choose the most suitable answer in each case. Mark it on your answer sheet.

1. Which of the following statements is true?
    A Henry VIII was the elder brother of Prince Arthur.
    B Elizabeth I was the mother of Henry VIII.
    C Henry VIII was the first son of Henry VII and Elizabeth of York.
    D Prince Arthur succeeded to the throne in 1502.
    E Henry VIII succeeded to the throne in 1509.

2. Which words best describe Henry?
    A athletic, sedentary, mathematical and religious
    B religious, thrifty, shy and academic
    C athletic, religious, musical and sociable
    D musical, artistic, religious and shy
    E sociable, dramatic, religious and quick-witted

3. Why would the Pope have been pleased that Henry attacked Martin Luther in his book?
    A Martin Luther was a defender of the Catholic Church.
    B Martin Luther was a Protestant priest who criticised the Catholic Church.
    C Martin Luther did not have the title Defender of the Faith.
    D The Pope was jealous of Martin Luther.
    E The Pope wanted Henry to be a staunch defender of the Protestant faith.

4. Which of these facts about Thomas Wolsey make it surprising that he managed to become 'one of the most influential ministers in British history'? (lines 39–40)
    A Wolsey was the son of an Ipswich butcher.
    B Wolsey became Lord Chancellor in 1515.
    C Wolsey built Hampton Court Palace.
    D Wolsey helped Henry to focus on government business.
    E Wolsey was often described as 'the other king'.

NOW GO ON TO THE NEXT PAGE

HENRY VIII

5. Wolsey was 'often described as "the other king"' (lines 40–41)

   What does this tell you about Wolsey?

   A He was Henry's best friend.

   B He was Henry's successor to the throne.

   C He was almost as powerful as Henry.

   D He stood in for Henry when Henry was ill.

   E He was king of Hampton Court Palace.

6. Why do you think Henry increased the size of the Navy so substantially?

   A To strengthen England's defences and his own power.

   B To show his love of ships and sailing at sea.

   C So he could sail to France or Spain whenever he wanted.

   D To impress Catherine of Aragon and his other wives.

   E To show that he had lots of money.

7. 'England had never had a ruling queen.' (line 64)

   What was one danger of having 'a ruling queen'?

   A A ruling queen might not produce any children.

   B A ruling queen might marry a foreigner which could weaken England's position of power.

   C No one believed a queen could do a good job of reigning.

   D A ruling queen might disgrace the royal family.

   E A ruling queen would never agree to marry a foreigner.

8. What reason did Henry give the Pope for wanting to annul his marriage to Catherine?

   A He no longer loved her.

   B She had been unfaithful to him.

   C She hadn't given him a son.

   D He had fallen in love with Anne Boleyn.

   E Their marriage was invalid because it was illegal.

9. What was the outcome of the English Reformation?

   A England embraced the Catholic Church.

   B England became a Protestant nation.

   C England had a ruling queen.

   D England named Cranmer as Archbishop of Canterbury.

   E Wolsey was replaced by Thomas Cromwell.

NOW GO ON TO THE NEXT PAGE

HENRY VIII

10. How was the annulment of Henry's marriage eventually achieved?
    A   The Pope relented and granted the annulment.
    B   Wolsey got the Pope to agree to a divorce.
    C   Cromwell threatened the Pope with excommunication.
    D   Cromwell proposed a change to who had the power to grant the annulment.
    E   Anne Boleyn persuaded the Pope to grant the annulment.

11. What did Henry do to deal with those who opposed him after the English Reformation?
    A   He passed the Act of Supremacy.
    B   He established the Church of England.
    C   He ordered the Dissolution of the Monasteries.
    D   He promoted Thomas Cranmer to Archbishop of Canterbury.
    E   He passed the Treasons Act.

12. What happened to the monasteries during the English Reformation?
    A   They were taken from the gentry and given to monks and priests.
    B   They were demolished, and the monks and priests were beheaded.
    C   They were sold to noblemen and their treasures seized.
    D   They were bought by Henry VIII who turned them into grand residences.
    E   They were sold to the Roman Catholic Church.

13. Why did Henry become popular with the nobility after the Dissolution of the Monasteries?
    A   The nobility had never liked the monks, nuns and friars.
    B   Henry put the nobility in charge of the Protestant Church.
    C   Henry allowed the nobility to keep the monks' treasures.
    D   Henry shared his profits with the nobility.
    E   Members of the nobility were able to buy the monasteries and land.

14. Which statement about Anne Boleyn is true?
    A   Anne Boleyn was able to provide Henry with a male heir.
    B   Henry's marriage to Anne Boleyn led to the establishment of the Church of England.
    C   Anne Boleyn was able to persuade the Pope to annul Henry's first marriage.
    D   Anne Boleyn was executed for giving birth to a girl.
    E   The Dissolution of the Monasteries was ordered by Anne Boleyn.

NOW GO ON TO THE NEXT PAGE

HENRY VIII

Now answer the following questions about the meanings of words as they are used in the passage.

15. 'As a reward for his staunch defence of the Catholic Church, the Pope gave Henry the title of Defender of the Faith.' (lines 25–27)

    Which is the closest in meaning to 'staunch'?

    A able

    B loyal

    C personal

    D royal

    E incredible

16. '… it could lead to a dispute about succession or to the domination of England by a foreign power through marriage.' (lines 67–70)

    Which is the closest in meaning to 'domination'?

    A connection

    B collapse

    C termination

    D formation

    E control

17. 'This was called the Dissolution of the Monasteries.' (lines 119–120)

    Which is the closest in meaning to 'dissolution'?

    A distribution

    B confiscation

    C resurgence

    D break-up

    E investigation

NOW GO ON TO THE NEXT PAGE

HENRY VIII

Now answer the following questions about words and phrases from the passage.

18. '... there was considerable risk associated with handing the Crown to a woman ...' (lines 65–67)

    Which word is an adjective?

    A considerable

    B risk

    C with

    D handing

    E woman

19. 'Cromwell ... decided that the monks, nuns and friars who resided in the country's many monasteries were corrupt, living in wealth and luxury unbecoming to their religious calling.' (lines 112–116)

    What type of words are 'wealth' and 'luxury'?

    A adjectives

    B adverbs

    C pronouns

    D abstract nouns

    E prepositions

20. '... Henry had a son, Edward, by his third wife' (line 133)

    What type of phrase is 'his third wife'?

    A prepositional phrase

    B expanded noun phrase

    C adjectival phrase

    D adverbial phrase

    E verb phrase

NOW GO ON TO THE NEXT PAGE

Walking with Polar Bears

Read this passage carefully, then answer the questions that follow.

Pop! goes the feeble sound from Andy MacPherson's pistol. We're standing less than 20 metres from a 600kg polar bear that is purposefully advancing on us. Her head down low, eyes fixed on mine, she's in a predatory trance as she lifts her muzzle and sniffs the air for my scent. Andy pulls the trigger twice more: *pop-pop!* Three duds in a row seems terribly unlucky and certainly not enough to deter a curious bear, but at least the minor commotion has taken the heat off me. Andy has valiantly put himself on the menu.

With a calm expression but jittering fingers, he scrambles to reload his gun from a fresh box of rounds, while his partner — tight-lipped Cree* naturalist, Albert 'Butch' Saunders — silently surveys the scene, the very definition of composure. This is the first time in over five years that Andy, a polar bear expert, has needed to fire a banger deterrent from his modified starter pistol… perhaps his ammunition, having sat idle for so long in his jacket pocket, has passed its sell-by date.

I remember the advice I received from Rose, a woman I met in Churchill — Canada's famous polar bear town — where the crack of special shotgun shells used to scare off inquisitive polar bears can be heard in the streets at night. If confronted with a bear, a) make yourself look big, b) don't turn your back on it, and c) move away slowly.

"Try to get into any building or car," Rose told me. "I couldn't even *tell* you where the keys to my house are. I'll go on a two-week vacation and leave my front door unlocked." Nobody locks anything in Churchill because they wouldn't want to rob anyone of an escape route.

However, we're 150 miles from Churchill now, so puffing up my chest to appear as large as possible, I glance over my shoulder at our purpose-built polar exploration vehicle: a hulking 4x4 powerhouse with huge wheels and seats bolted to it, dubbed 'the rhino'. Unfortunately, it has neither doors nor roof, so while it offers panoramic views of the night skies, it won't provide much protection from an eight-foot bear this morning.

Steam rises from the nearby lake and arctic strawberries shine like rubies from the verdant summer undergrowth, hung with dew-bejewelled spiders' webs. It's a scene of beauty, making the approaching white bear seem somehow immaterial. But the bear, and the danger, are very real.

Andy usually discourages polar bears from approaching us simply by talking to them or clicking a couple of rocks together — methods with which I've already seen him repel investigative bears — but Andy's chatter goes unheeded this time. Butch remains mute.

Flanked by two experts, armed with shotguns and firecrackers, I'm sure I'm in safe company, though. To be honest, I'm relishing the opportunity to study her up close. Her unique physiology — slightly webbed toes and musculature across her chest designed for swimming — defines her species as the world's only marine bear.

Even as she stalks us, she looks adorable, but I realise the situation has escalated when hawk-eyed Albert bursts into life and launches a few stones towards the bear. They explode like waterbombs in the puddles around her and she retreats, momentarily startled, before fear turns to annoyance and she perseveres with her approach.

Albert jumps into the rhino and aggressively revs the engine, making the vehicle lurch forward. Despite his ballistic assault on the polar bear, she barely breaks stride, and as soon as he kills the motor her attention is again fixed solely on us.

Bang! A projectile rockets from the barrel of Andy's starter pistol. The low-powered round arcs through the air with the force of a lobbed tennis ball and bursts mere inches from our polar bear's brow. It makes my ears ring where *I'm* standing, so the bear must be deafened and, with a thunderclap that covers her head in a cloud of smoke, she finally flees.

As Andy bins his spent cartridges and pours us coffee from a flask, I spy Albert's redundant shotgun sitting idle in the rhino, and note the absence of a pistol on his hip.

"Sure I have one," he smiles over the brim of his mug, and produces a gleaming, immaculate starting gun from a pristine leatherette case. "I've had it for over ten years."

"When did you last have to use yours?" I ask him.

He smirks in a way that silently indicates extensive knowledge of wildlife gathered over thousands of years, and replies, "Never."

*The Cree is one of the largest First Nations groups in Canada.

WALKING WITH POLAR BEARS

Now answer these questions, looking at the passage again if you need to. Choose the most suitable answer in each case. Mark it on your answer sheet.

21. What creates a sense of danger in the first paragraph?

    A   The pop of the pistol fired by Andy MacPherson.

    B   The men's proximity to a huge polar bear that is coming towards them.

    C   The polar bear's curiosity at the sight of human beings.

    D   The polar bear keeping her head down low.

    E   Andy looking forward to the lunchtime menu.

22. '*Pop!* goes the feeble sound from Andy MacPherson's pistol.' (lines 1–2)

    What does this tell you about Andy's pistol?

    A   It hasn't made the loud noise that was expected.

    B   It is a toy pistol that he uses for fun.

    C   It creates a really loud sound.

    D   It hasn't been used for a long time.

    E   It provides the men with protection.

23. What is good for the writer about the 'minor commotion' created by Andy MacPherson? (line 11)

    A   The polar bear comes out of her predatory trance.

    B   The polar bear runs away.

    C   The polar bear's interest switches from the author to Andy.

    D   Andy realises his pistol needs repairing.

    E   The polar bear lifts her muzzle and sniffs the air.

24. Which one of these statements is true?

    A   In Churchill, everyone locks their doors.

    B   Andy MacPherson frequently uses a firearm to scare off bears.

    C   The author met Rose when on holiday in Vancouver.

    D   The author is a well-known polar bear expert.

    E   The Cree is a First Nations group in Canada.

NOW GO ON TO THE NEXT PAGE

WALKING WITH POLAR BEARS

25. 'Andy has valiantly put himself on the menu.' (lines 12–13)
    What does the writer mean by this?
    A Andy likes to eat bear.
    B Andy could now be eaten by the bear.
    C Andy has asked for the lunch menu.
    D Andy doesn't know what to do next.
    E Andy isn't confident he can beat the bear.

26. What do the words 'jittering' and 'scrambles' tell you about Andy? (lines 14–15)
    A He is nervous and in a rush.
    B He is cold and in a rush.
    C He is nervous but enjoying himself.
    D He is calm but nervous.
    E He is nervous and off-balance.

27. What does 'the very definition of composure' tell you about Albert Saunders? (line 19)
    A He is tight-lipped.
    B He is a naturalist.
    C He is calm.
    D He is surveying the scene.
    E He is jittery.

28. What is the purpose of Andy's 'modified starter pistol'? (line 22)
    A To kill an advancing polar bear.
    B To announce the start of a race.
    C To give him more confidence.
    D To show the others he is in charge.
    E To deter an advancing polar bear.

WALKING WITH POLAR BEARS

29. What advice did Rose give the author about what to do when faced with a polar bear?
    1 Make yourself look big.
    2 Turn around and run away as fast as you can.
    3 Curl into a ball while keeping eye contact.
    4 Scream loudly to scare off the bear.
    5 Don't turn your back but move slowly away.
    A 1 and 2
    B 1 and 5
    C 3 and 5
    D 2 and 5
    E 4 and 5

30. Why is nothing locked in Churchill?
    A They are all friends and family.
    B There is absolutely no crime there.
    C So that people can escape attacking bears.
    D To encourage people to interact with bears.
    E To encourage bears to approach humans.

31. Why might the team's exploration vehicle be dubbed 'the rhino'? (line 47)
    A Because it is huge and powerful.
    B Because it is often used to capture rhinoceros.
    C Because it has a horn on the bonnet.
    D Because they are in rhinoceros territory.
    E To show how much protection it provides.

32. What contrasts with the danger posed by the polar bear?
    A Andy clicking a couple of rocks together.
    B The steam from the lake.
    C The beauty of the lake and arctic strawberries.
    D Andy's constant chattering.
    E The panoramic views of the night skies.

NOW GO ON TO THE NEXT PAGE

WALKING WITH POLAR BEARS

33. What is the polar bear's reaction when Albert revs the rhino's engine?
    A   She isn't particularly bothered.
    B   She strides off into the distance.
    C   She attacks the rhino.
    D   She lurches forwards.
    E   She stands tall and beats her chest.

34. What finally makes the polar bear run off?
    A   The tennis ball which has been lobbed through the air.
    B   The sound of thunder and lightning.
    C   Albert's ballistic assault on the polar bear.
    D   The deafening sound of a banger fired from Andy's pistol.
    E   The sound of the rhino's engine being revved.

35. What indicates that Albert is an expert on how to deal with bears?
    A   He produces his starter pistol.
    B   He has never had to use his gun.
    C   He keeps his gun in a leatherette case.
    D   He keeps his gun in the rhino.
    E   He is a Cree.

WALKING WITH POLAR BEARS

Now answer the following questions about the meanings of words as they are used in the passage.

36. Which word is the closest in meaning to 'redundant'? (line 99)
    A sturdy
    B professional
    C illegal
    D unnecessary
    E flimsy

37. Which word is the closest in meaning to 'pristine'? (line 103)
    A hand-made
    B immaculate
    C natural
    D scruffy
    E handsome

Now answer the following questions about words and phrases from the passage.

38. '… arctic strawberries shine like rubies from the verdant summer undergrowth' (lines 53–54)
    How is this clause best described?
    A simile
    B metaphor
    C personification
    D onomatopoeia
    E rhetoric

39. '… I'm relishing the opportunity to study her up close.' (lines 69–70)
    What type of phrase is 'up close'?
    A adjectival phrase
    B expanded noun phrase
    C adverbial phrase
    D verbal phrase
    E noun phrase

40. 'As Andy bins his spent cartridges and pours us coffee from a flask …' (lines 97–98)
    Which word is a verb?
    A bins   B spent   C cartridges   D from   E flask

NOW GO ON TO THE NEXT PAGE

SPELLING EXERCISE

In the following passage, there are some spelling mistakes. On each numbered line you will see that there is either one mistake or no mistake. Find the group of words with the mistake in it and mark its letter on your answer sheet. If there is no mistake, mark the letter N.

The Shooting of Archduke Ferdinand

41. Earlier today, **(A)** while visiting **(B)** Serbia on offitial **(C)** business, Archduke **(D)** Ferdinand

42. of Austria-Hungary **(A)** was assasinated **(B)** as his driver **(C)** stopped outside **(D)** a shop to ask for

43. directions. **(A)** A terrorist emerged **(B)** from the premises, **(C)** weilding a pistol **(D)** and proceeded to

44. take aim **(A)** at the Archduke. **(B)** The shot entered the Archduke's **(C)** neck above his **(D)** protective vest

45. and he died instantly. **(A)** Immediatley after, **(B)** the Archduke's **(C)** wife was fatally shot **(D)** in the

46. stomack. **(A)** A member of the **(B)** Black Hand terrorist group, **(C)** nineteen-year-old **(D)** Bosnian

47. Gavrilo Princip, **(A)** was arrested on the spot **(B)** and torchured **(C)** by police officers **(D)** until he

48. reveeled the names **(A)** of his fellow gang members. **(B)** The case **(C)** will be brought

(D) before the courts in due course.

WORD SELECTION EXERCISE

In the following passage, you have to pick the most appropriate word or group of words so that the passage makes sense. Choose one of the five answers on each line and mark its letter on your answer sheet.

In the Deep, Dark Jungle

49. Deep in the dark green heart of the jungle, | lurks (A) | lurking (B) | lurk (C) | is lurking (D) | was lurking (E) |

50. many mysterious and majestic creatures. | Or (A) | From (B) | With (C) | On (D) | After (E) | snakes to

51. spiders, gorillas to iguanas, parrots to panthers, it is | this (A) | some (B) | that (C) | a (D) | any (E) | paradise

52. for wildlife lovers. Dangling vines brush the leafy floor | as (A) | for (B) | with (C) | so (D) | because (E) |

53. chimps chase each other and | swung (A) | swang (B) | is swinging (C) | swings (D) | swing (E) | mischievously

54. in the canopy that towers | above (A) | below (B) | beside (C) | under (D) | aside (E) |. Their screeches echo far

55. and wide and sound as if murder is being | admitted (A) | committed (B) | had (C) | finished (D) | did (E) |.

56. The squawking sound of parrots | finds (A) | stills (B) | fills (C) | comes (D) | forms (E) | the air.

END OF TEST

Collins
PRACTICE PAPERS

Answers and Explanations

English

Practice Paper A Answers and Explanations

1. **B**
   The sentence suggests that Mary hasn't found anything in her life very interesting up to now.
2. **C**
   The repetition of 'she skipped' reflects Mary's continuous or repeated skipping in various parts of the garden.
3. **E**
   At the end of the first paragraph, the narrator says: 'She had wondered if he would notice her. She wanted him to see her skip.' This suggests she thinks she is skipping well as she wouldn't want anyone to see her if she wasn't sure of her ability.
4. **B**
   The narrator writes: 'The sun was shining and a little wind was blowing—not a rough wind, but one which came in delightful little gusts …' (lines 10–13)
5. **E**
   Ben had thought Mary was 'sour' which can mean morose or disagreeable. However, he is now seeing her in a different light as she is skipping and behaving like a happy child.
6. **A**
   Ben states that the robin is a curious creature and suggests that he will follow Mary to find out what a skipping-rope is as he's never seen one.
7. **D**
   The narrator says: 'She did not mind much, because she had already counted up to thirty.' As this is ten more skips than she had previously achieved, she was happy to stop.
8. **C**
   Later on, in line 103, the narrator says: '… she put her hand in her pocket, drew out the key …'
9. **B**
   In line 61 we are told that Mary 'laughed again' when she saw that the robin had followed her. This suggests she is happy to see him, especially as he may be able to help her find the door.
10. **D**
    In lines 69–71, the narrator says: 'Nothing in the world is quite as adorably lovely as a robin when he shows off …' in reference to his 'lovely trill' which refers to a bird's song.
11. **E**
    Mary is referring to the fact that the wind had surged enough to cause the ivy to swing aside and expose the door.
12. **B**
    In paragraph one, we are told that Ben was digging in the kitchen-garden which is something that a gardener would do.
13. **B**
    We are told in lines 94–96 that 'Mary's heart began to thump and her hands to shake a little in her delight and excitement.'
14. **D**
    The question in lines 99–101, 'What was this under her hands which was square and made of iron and which her fingers found a hole in?' is answered in the next line: 'It was the lock of the door …'
15. **A**
    The lock would have been stiff because it had been 'closed ten years' so it would be hard for a child to turn; using two hands would make it easier.
16. **C**
    Although the text does not say explicitly that Mary did not want to be seen going through the door, it is inferred by the way she 'slipped' through the door and shut it behind her, suggesting that she didn't want anyone to see that the door had been opened.
17. **B**
    Ben speaks in a local dialect. It is clear from the context that 'tha'' and 'thee' mean you.
18. **A**
    The word 'heathen' can be used to describe someone who doesn't believe in God; 'pagan' is a synonym for heathen.
19. **E**
    'Look sharp' means 'hurry up'.
20. **C**
    The word 'chirp' is used to describe the noise a bird makes, as is 'twitter'.
21. **D**
    Ben is saying that despite having lived in India ('lived with heathen'), Mary is doing well with her skipping.
22. **D**
    Personification is when a human characteristic is given to a non-human object.
23. **A**
    'It' is a pronoun, used here to replace the word 'wind'.
24. **B**
    A metaphor is a figure of speech that describes something by saying it is something else. Here, the ivy is being described as 'a loose and swinging curtain'.
25. **E**
    Here, the word 'iron' is a noun. Although 'square' can be a noun, in this context it is used as an adjective.
26. **B**
    The misspelt word in the group is 'dammage' which should be 'damage'.
27. **D**
    The misspelt word in the group is 'rediculously' which should be 'ridiculously'.
28. **B**
    The misspelt word in the group is 'summat' which should be 'summit'.
29. **A**
    The misspelt word in the group is 'furneture' which should be 'furniture'.
30. **C**
    The misspelt word in the group is 'poring' which should be 'pouring'.
31. **C**
    The misspelt word in the group is 'ashored' which should be 'assured'.
32. **N**
    There are no misspelt words in these groups.
33. **A**
    The misspelt word in the group is 'nieghbour's' which should be 'neighbour's'.

34. **A**
   The contraction of 'she had' is 'she'd', where the apostrophe indicates the missing 'ha'.
35. **N**
   There is no incorrect punctuation in these groups.
36. **C**
   There should be a full stop after 'moorland' as it is the end of the sentence.
37. **B**
   There should be a comma after 'that' and before the final inverted comma/speech mark at the end of the direct speech.
38. **B**
   There should be an inverted comma/speech mark after 'haystack.' to indicate the end of the direct speech.
39. **D**
   There should be an apostrophe before the 's' in 'Gemmas' to indicate possession: 'Gemma's heart'.
40. **D**
   There should be either a colon or a dash after 'trouble' to separate the two clauses.
41. **B**
   There should be a bracket after 'Dad!'.
42. **D**
   The simple past tense of the verb 'fly' is 'flew'. None of the other words make sense.
43. **A**
   The simple past tense of the verb 'sit' is 'sat'. None of the other verb forms make sense.
44. **B**
   The preposition 'for' comes after 'tease him'.
45. **C**
   The pronoun 'he' refers to Karl; the passage is written in the third person singular.
46. **B**
   The modal verb 'might' is the only one that makes sense.
47. **B**
   The only word that makes sense is 'again'.
48. **C**
   The only noun that makes sense is 'eyes'.
49. **E**
   The only verb that makes sense is 'staring'.

Practice Paper B Answers and Explanations

1. **C**
   Jen sees 'the roads gnarled and choked by rusted hulks of cars and trucks, and the gradual advance of decades-old vegetation' (lines 4–6) which does not suggest a pulsating, living city.
2. **B**
   Jen's father has told her the same story many times and he is curious about why she wants to hear it again.
3. **B**
   The narrator says, 'Jen always marvelled at how graceful he was.' (lines 22–23)
4. **E**
   Jen compares her father to a series of pictures of a man dancing.
5. **D**
   In some pictures, the dancing man 'crouched'.
6. **B**
   The word 'condensed' means to reduce or compress. Jen's father has condensed the story but Jen knows this because she has heard the story before.
7. **A**
   Jen sighs in frustration as she knows her father is trying to fob her off with the short version of the story.
8. **D**
   Jen's father says that humanity's destruction of their habitat was a 'slow method, a method so gradual that humanity as a whole didn't notice at first.' (lines 56–58)
9. **B**
   In saying 'Humans make no sense,' Jen's father has generalised. Jen is letting him know that as she is human, his criticism is of her too. 'narrowing your eyes' means looking at someone in a serious or cross way.
10. **C**
    The thought that a child may have owned the toy rabbit makes Jen feel uneasy as they may have died.
11. **A**
    The Flood happened after a short circuit in the Hive system which caused machines to fail and people with microchips in their heads to die a painful death. This was clearly a distressing part of the tale to tell Jen.
12. **E**
    Following the destruction of the world, there would presumably have been an end to education so Jen's father is wondering where she has heard about the Dark Ages.
13. **C**
    'Jen wanted to say … *Maybe one day after you've told it to me often enough, I'll begin to understand it …*' (lines 112–115)
14. **B**
    Jen follows this gesture with the words: 'Book learning.' to let her father know she has read about the Dark Ages. The tap to the side of her head is a reference to her being clever.
15. **C**
    Gnarled can mean twisted or knotted.
16. **E**
    To pirouette is to spin, turn or whirl.
17. **E**
    In essence means basically or essentially.
18. **D**
    Melding is a noun formed from the verb meld.
19. **A**
    They are adjectives. Adjectives provide more information about nouns.
20. **E**
    A simile is a figure of speech that expresses the resemblance of one thing to another, usually introduced by 'as' or 'like'.
21. **D**
    The misspelt word in the group is 'cobbelstone' which should be 'cobblestone'.
22. **D**
    The misspelt word in the group is 'glimse' which should be 'glimpse'.
23. **C**
    The misspelt word in the group is 'narled' which should be 'gnarled'.

24. **C**
   The misspelt word in the group is 'abundence' which should be 'abundance'.
25. **B**
   The misspelt word in the group is 'dazzeling' which should be 'dazzling'.
26. **N**
   There are no misspelt words in these groups.
27. **A**
   The misspelt word in the group is 'tresures' which should be 'treasures'.
28. **B**
   The misspelt word in the group is 'lazely' which should be 'lazily'.
29. **A**
   The misspelt word in the group is 'marmelade' which should be 'marmalade'.
30. **D**
   The misspelt word in the group is 'there' which should be 'their'.
31. **B**
   The misspelt word in the group is 'dropplets' which should be 'droplets'.
32. **B**
   The misspelt word in the group is 'welcomeing' which should be 'welcoming'.
33. **C**
   The colon should come after 'fruit' to introduce the list of fruit he buys.
34. **B**
   The comma should come after 'goal', which indicates the end of the subordinate clause.
35. **D**
   A full stop is missing from the end of the sentence.
36. **A**
   The contraction of 'have not' is written 'haven't', where the apostrophe indicates the missing 'o'.
37. **C**
   There should be an apostrophe before the 's' in 'Mayas' to indicate possession: 'Maya's house'.
38. **B**
   'Ireland' is a proper noun (it is the name of a country) which means it starts with a capital letter.
39. **N**
   There is no incorrect punctuation in these groups.
40. **C**
   As Zac has asked a question, there should be a question mark after 'match', not a comma.
41. **A**
   There should be an apostrophe in the contraction 'There's' to indicate where the missing 'i' should be in 'There is'.
42. **C**
   There should be a closing bracket after 'activity' to indicate the end of the words in parenthesis.
43. **A**
   The word 'summer' is not a proper noun and does not start with a capital letter.
44. **C**
   There should be a semi-colon or a single dash after 'pond' to separate the two independent clauses.
45. **B**
   No other word makes sense.
46. **A**
   The simple past tense of 'take' is 'took'.
47. **D**
   The preposition 'about' is needed after 'they told each other a little'.
48. **C**
   The subordinating conjunction 'while' is the only word which makes sense.
49. **B**
   The simple past tense of 'be' is 'was'.
50. **D**
   The preposition 'through' is needed after 'peeked'.
51. **B**
   The modal verb 'wouldn't' is the only word which makes sense.
52. **E**
   No other word makes sense.
53. **D**
   'To get a clip round the ear' is a phrase meaning to be given a light slap around the head.
54. **A**
   The correct preposition is 'from'.
55. **A**
   'To have ideas above your station' is a phrase meaning to have aspirations above your social position.
56. **E**
   No other word makes sense.

Practice Paper C Answers and Explanations

1. **D**
   The narrator says: '… he was an important man, which meant he could afford a big house on the Esquiline Hill.' (lines 7–9)
2. **B**
   After the words 'Lucius's room', the word *cubiculum* is written in italics which indicates that this is the Roman word.
3. **E**
   There is a shrine to the household Gods in the *atrium* and the dining room walls are covered in pictures of the Gods.
4. **D**
   The faint buzzing sound is the 'city's constant background noise'.
5. **E**
   As slaves, they were standing out of sight until their master and mistress called for them: 'waiting to do the bidding of their master and mistress.' (lines 37–38)
6. **C**
   Lucius knows that Gaius is an important man which would have made him anxious, so he has practised his words in an effort to get them right.
7. **E**
   His father had turned out to be a drinker and gambler, losing most of his money. This led to bitter arguments.
8. **B**
   The narrator says: 'Lucius knew his mother wasn't unhappy when his father died, mourning him only because it was expected.' (lines 65–68)

9. **B**
The narrator says: 'If you wanted to reach the top in Rome, you had to be connected to one of the ancient families – by birth, or at least by marriage.' (lines 92–95)

10. **C**
He tips his head to one side, as though considering the request, then studies Lucius, suggesting he is thinking calmly.

11. **D**
Lucius feels like a lodger in Gaius's house rather than a son or member of the family. If he were to be adopted by him, he would have the same rights as a son which would give him security.

12. **B**
He knows he has to choose the right words in his response to Gaius. If he were to get it wrong, his life could take a completely different turn.

13. **A**
Lucius had said 'I want to be like you' (line 134) which would have appealed to Gaius's ego and made him smile with satisfaction.

14. **E**
The narrator says that 'both Lucius's grandfathers had long since died, and he had no living uncles, no older brothers who could give him advice or introductions to men who might help him. There were not even any male friends of the family.' (lines 149–154)

15. **C**
Lucius's father was a drinker and a gambler; it is inferred that this meant his behaviour had alienated any male friends he might once have had.

16. **A**
The phrase 'to do the bidding of' means to carry out the wishes of someone.

17. **E**
The adjective 'noble' can mean belonging to a high social class and having a title. 'Aristocratic' can have the same meaning.

18. **B**
A cubicle is a small partitioned-off area of a room and Lucius's *cubiculum* was his partitioned-off area of the house.

19. **D**
The adjective 'slender' can mean slim or slight.

20. **A**
When used to refer to eyes, hazel means greenish-brown in colour.

21. **C**
A simile is a figure of speech that expresses the resemblance of one thing to another, usually introduced by 'as' or 'like'.

22. **A**
An adjective provides more information about a noun. 'Watchful' describes Gaius's gaze.

23. **D**
A verb can describe an action or a state of being or having.

24. **E**
The subjunctive mood is a verb form which can be used to express a suggestion or hypothetical scenario.

25. **A**
An adverbial phrase can provide more information about a verb, another adverb or an adjective. It can tell you when, where, how or how often something happens. Here, it is *when* Lucius's father died.

26. **B**
The misspelt word in the group is 'conference' which should be 'conference'.

27. **A**
The misspelt word in the group is 'harty' which should be 'hearty'.

28. **C**
The misspelt word in the group is 'stationary' which should be 'stationery'.

29. **B**
The misspelt word in the group is 'condolances' which should be 'condolences'.

30. **N**
There are no misspelt words in these groups.

31. **B**
The misspelt word in the group is 'fatige' which should be 'fatigue'.

32. **D**
The misspelt word in the group is 'exagerate' which should be 'exaggerate'.

33. **A**
The misspelt word in the group is 'gestered' which should be 'gestured'.

34. **B**
The comma should come after 'Chloe' not after 'pointing'.

35. **D**
There should be a full stop after 'added'.

36. **D**
There should be either a full stop or an exclamation mark after 'water', not a question mark.

37. **A**
The word 'you' should start with a capital Y because it starts a sentence.

38. **A**
There is an apostrophe missing in the word 'lets' to indicate a contraction of 'let us'.

39. **N**
There is no incorrect punctuation in these groups.

40. **B**
There should be a hyphen between 'get' and 'togethers' as this is a compound noun.

41. **B**
There should be a closing bracket after the score '3 – 0'.

42. **C**
No other word makes sense.

43. **E**
No other word makes sense.

44. **B**
No other word makes sense.

45. **A**
No other word makes sense.

46. **A**
No other word makes sense.

47. **C**
The adverbial 'In spite' would only make sense if followed by 'of'. Only 'Despite' makes sense.

48. **B**
No other word makes sense. 'plaice' (a type of fish) and 'place' (position) are homophones.

49. **D**
No other word makes sense. 'peek' (a quick look) and 'peak' (a high point) are homophones.

Practice Paper D Answers and Explanations

1. **E**
   Henry VIII succeeded to the throne in 1509. He became heir when his older brother died in 1502 but became king when his father died.
2. **C**
   Henry liked hunting, jousting and playing tennis: athletic. He attended mass regularly: religious. He was skilled in playing many musical instruments: musical. He held lavish parties: sociable.
3. **B**
   The Pope and Henry were Catholics, while Martin Luther was a Protestant who had criticised the Catholic Church.
4. **A**
   It would have been unusual at this time in history for someone with such humble origins ('the son of an Ipswich butcher') to be able to become so powerful.
5. **C**
   Being referred to as 'the other king' suggests that Henry relied on Wolsey when making decisions and implies that he was almost as powerful as the king.
6. **A**
   As the ruler of an island, it would be important to have good defences in place. Also, it would send a message to potential attackers that England had a strong defence force.
7. **B**
   If a ruling queen were to marry someone from a foreign country, this foreign power could dominate England and weaken England's position.
8. **E**
   Henry asserted that his marriage to Catherine of Aragon had never been legal and therefore should be annulled.
9. **B**
   England broke away from the Catholic Church and became Protestant.
10. **D**
    Cromwell resolved the problem by giving Parliament rather than the Pope the authority to grant the annulment.
11. **E**
    The Treasons Act meant that anyone who questioned Henry's power over the Church could be accused of treason and punished by death.
12. **C**
    The Dissolution of the Monasteries involved closing down the monasteries, selling them to the nobility and seizing the treasures amassed by the monks.
13. **E**
    The nobility were pleased that, thanks to Henry, they were able to buy the monasteries (and the land) and turn them into grand residences for themselves.
14. **B**
    The establishment of the Church of England came about because Henry wanted to divorce Catherine of Aragon so he could marry Anne Boleyn. This could not happen while England was under the Catholic Church so Henry had to break away from the Pope and establish the Church of England.
15. **B**
    A staunch believer is very loyal to a person or a set of beliefs and supports them strongly.
16. **E**
    Here, domination means control or rule by a foreign power.
17. **D**
    Dissolution can mean the end or break-up of something. The monasteries as they had been (inhabited by monks, nuns and friars living in luxury) were finished.
18. **A**
    An adjective modifies or describes a noun or pronoun. Here, 'considerable' gives more information about the noun 'risk'.
19. **D**
    An abstract noun is a word that names emotions, feelings, ideas or concepts (such as wealth, luxury, love, hate), unlike a common noun which is a 'concrete' object (such as dog, chair, table, pen).
20. **B**
    An expanded noun phrase is a group of words that includes a noun and at least one adjective to describe it.
21. **B**
    The men are 'less than 20 metres from a 600kg polar bear that is purposefully advancing' (lines 2–4) on them. In giving the distance from and the weight of the polar bear, and the fact that it is moving towards them, the writer creates a sense of danger.
22. **A**
    The word 'feeble' means weak; Andy's pistol hasn't made the expected loud noise.
23. **C**
    The author says, '… at least the minor commotion has taken the heat off me' which means the bear has switched its attention away from him and onto Andy.
24. **E**
    There is an asterisk (*) against the word 'Cree' in the second paragraph which indicates that the word will be explained in a footnote at the end of the text. The explanation is given as: *The Cree is one of the largest First Nations groups in Canada.*
25. **B**
    In saying that 'Andy has valiantly [bravely] put himself on the menu', the writer suggests that now the bear's attention has switched to Andy, he is the new target and could be eaten as though he were a dish on a menu.
26. **A**
    'jittering fingers' suggests Andy is nervous, and 'scrambles' suggests he rushes to put more rounds into his gun.
27. **C**
    To display composure means to display calmness. To say Albert is 'the very definition of composure' emphasises this calm; in other words, he embodies the very essence of composure.
28. **E**
    In this context, 'to deter' means to frighten off. The 'modified starter pistol' is not intended to kill polar bears; it is a starter pistol, which has been altered (modified) to fire a projectile to frighten bears off, not bullets to kill.

29. **B**
The author reveals that Rose has told him to do the following if confronted with a bear: a) make yourself look big (1), b) don't turn your back on it, and c) move away slowly (5).
30. **C**
The residents of Churchill want to allow each other the chance of an 'escape route' should they be approached by a polar bear. This means they leave their doors unlocked so people can have access, if necessary.
31. **A**
The vehicle is described as 'hulking' and a 'powerhouse' which means it is big and strong like a rhinoceros.
32. **C**
The beautiful description of the lake and the arctic strawberries is a striking contrast to the danger posed by the approaching polar bear.
33. **A**
The author says that the polar bear 'barely breaks stride' (line 85), which means she hardly reacts.
34. **D**
When Andy's pistol works properly, it makes a deafening sound and fires a banger.
35. **B**
The fact that Albert has never had to use his gun suggests that he has alternative methods to frighten off polar bears and knows what he is doing.
36. **D**
The word 'redundant' in this context means 'unnecessary' or 'surplus to requirements'. Albert would appear to prefer other means of scaring off polar bears.
37. **B**
The word 'pristine' can mean extremely clean (immaculate) or new.
38. **A**
A simile is a figure of speech that expresses the resemblance of one thing to another, usually introduced by 'as' or 'like'.
39. **C**
An adverbial phrase is two or more words that function like an adverb to modify a verb, adjective, adverb or even a whole sentence. Here, 'up close' modifies the verb 'study'.
40. **A**
A verb can describe an action or a state of being or having. 'bins' is what Andy does/the action he carries out.
41. **C**
The misspelt word in the group is 'offitial' which should be 'official'.
42. **B**
The misspelt word in the group is 'assasinated' which should be 'assassinated'.
43. **C**
The misspelt word in the group is 'weilding' which should be 'wielding'.
44. **N**
There are no misspelt words in these groups.
45. **B**
The misspelt word in the group is 'Immediatley' which should be 'Immediately'.
46. **A**
The misspelt word in the group is 'stomack' which should be 'stomach'.
47. **C**
The misspelt word in the group is 'torchured' which should be 'tortured'.
48. **A**
The misspelt word in the group is 'reveeled' which should be 'revealed'.
49. **C**
'lurk' is the present tense, third-person plural of the verb 'lurk'.
50. **B**
No other word makes sense.
51. **D**
No other word makes sense.
52. **A**
No other word makes sense.
53. **E**
'swing' is the present tense, third-person plural of the verb 'swing'.
54. **A**
No other word makes sense. (The canopy 'towers' so it must be above.)
55. **B**
A murder is committed.
56. **C**
No other word makes sense.

EN A

Pupil's Name	
School Name	

Date of Test

Please mark like this ⊢⊣.

PUPIL NUMBER

[0]	[0]	[0]	[0]	[0]	[0]
[1]	[1]	[1]	[1]	[1]	[1]
[2]	[2]	[2]	[2]	[2]	[2]
[3]	[3]	[3]	[3]	[3]	[3]
[4]	[4]	[4]	[4]	[4]	[4]
[5]	[5]	[5]	[5]	[5]	[5]
[6]	[6]	[6]	[6]	[6]	[6]
[7]	[7]	[7]	[7]	[7]	[7]
[8]	[8]	[8]	[8]	[8]	[8]
[9]	[9]	[9]	[9]	[9]	[9]

SCHOOL NUMBER

[0]	[0]	[0]	[0]	[0]	[0]	[0]
[1]	[1]	[1]	[1]	[1]	[1]	[1]
[2]	[2]	[2]	[2]	[2]	[2]	[2]
[3]	[3]	[3]	[3]	[3]	[3]	[3]
[4]	[4]	[4]	[4]	[4]	[4]	[4]
[5]	[5]	[5]	[5]	[5]	[5]	[5]
[6]	[6]	[6]	[6]	[6]	[6]	[6]
[7]	[7]	[7]	[7]	[7]	[7]	[7]
[8]	[8]	[8]	[8]	[8]	[8]	[8]
[9]	[9]	[9]	[9]	[9]	[9]	[9]

DATE OF BIRTH

Day		Month	Year
[0]	[0]	January	2011
[1]	[1]	February	2012
[2]	[2]	March	2013
[3]	[3]	April	2014
	[4]	May	2015
	[5]	June	2016
	[6]	July	2017
	[7]	August	2018
	[8]	September	2019
	[9]	October	2020
		November	2021
		December	2022

The Secret Garden

1 A B C D E
2 A B C D E
3 A B C D E
4 A B C D E
5 A B C D E
6 A B C D E
7 A B C D E
8 A B C D E
9 A B C D E
10 A B C D E
11 A B C D E
12 A B C D E
13 A B C D E
14 A B C D E
15 A B C D E
16 A B C D E
17 A B C D E
18 A B C D E
19 A B C D E
20 A B C D E
21 A B C D E
22 A B C D E
23 A B C D E
24 A B C D E
25 A B C D E

Spelling

26 A B C D N
27 A B C D N
28 A B C D N
29 A B C D N
30 A B C D N
31 A B C D N
32 A B C D N
33 A B C D N

Punctuation: No Time to Lose

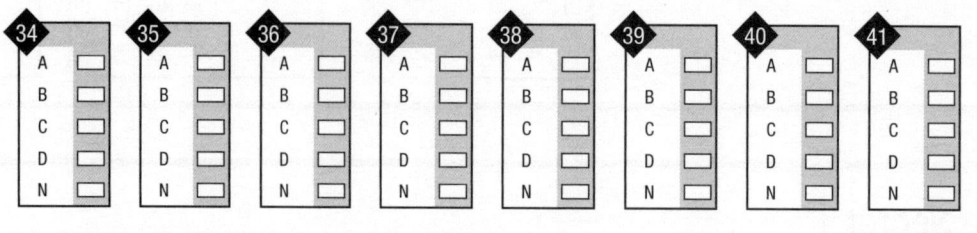

Word Selection: Freddy Makes an Observation

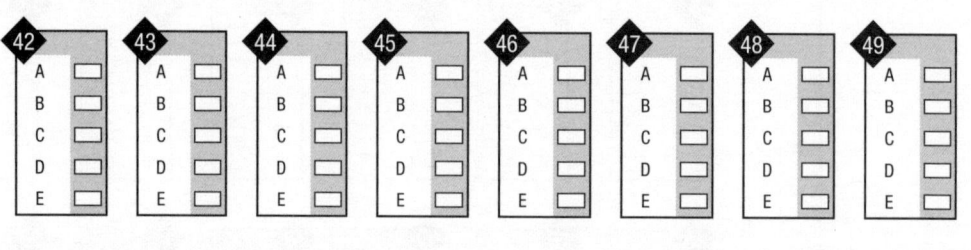

ENGLISH TEST B

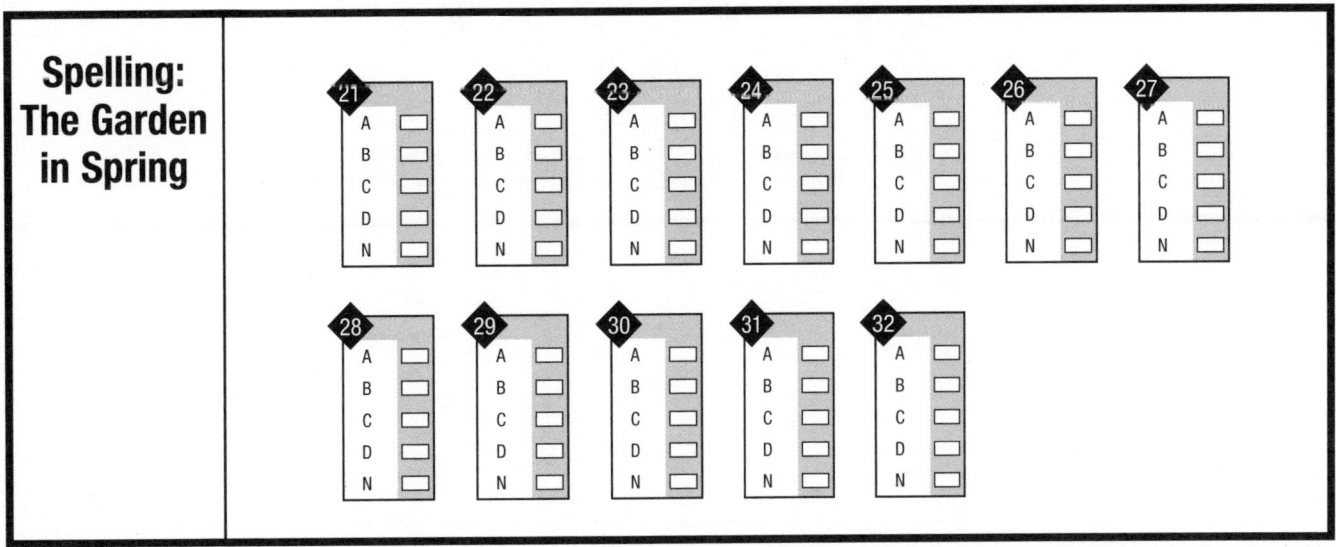

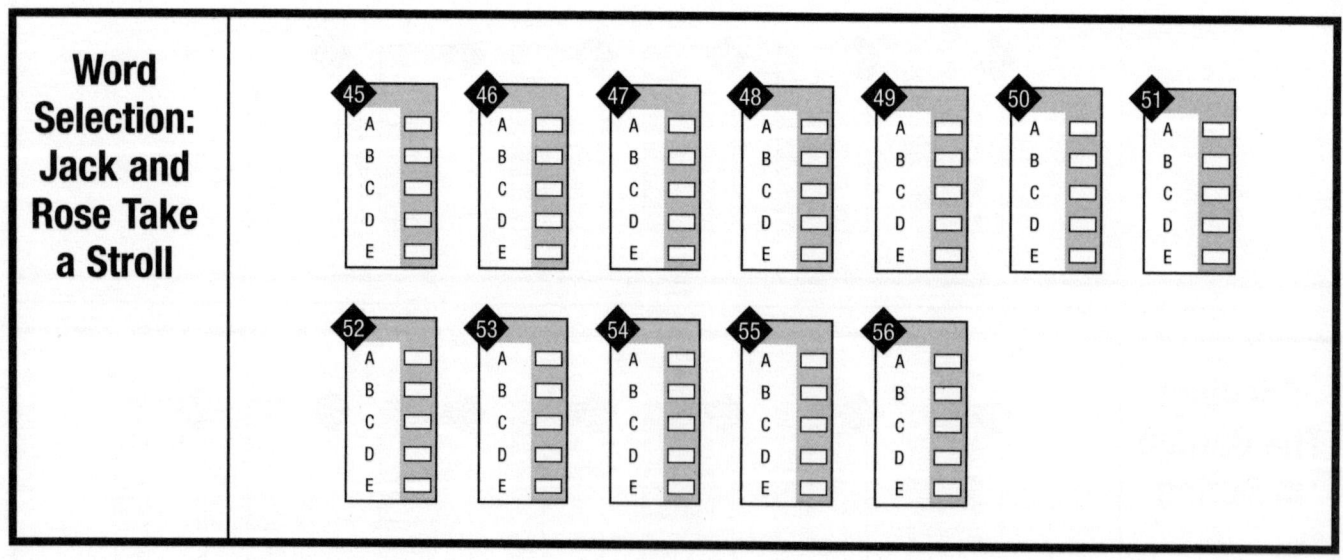

Pupil's Name

Date of Test

School Name

Please mark like this ⊟.

PUPIL NUMBER

[0]	[0]	[0]	[0]	[0]	[0]
[1]	[1]	[1]	[1]	[1]	[1]
[2]	[2]	[2]	[2]	[2]	[2]
[3]	[3]	[3]	[3]	[3]	[3]
[4]	[4]	[4]	[4]	[4]	[4]
[5]	[5]	[5]	[5]	[5]	[5]
[6]	[6]	[6]	[6]	[6]	[6]
[7]	[7]	[7]	[7]	[7]	[7]
[8]	[8]	[8]	[8]	[8]	[8]
[9]	[9]	[9]	[9]	[9]	[9]

SCHOOL NUMBER

[0]	[0]	[0]	[0]	[0]	[0]	[0]
[1]	[1]	[1]	[1]	[1]	[1]	[1]
[2]	[2]	[2]	[2]	[2]	[2]	[2]
[3]	[3]	[3]	[3]	[3]	[3]	[3]
[4]	[4]	[4]	[4]	[4]	[4]	[4]
[5]	[5]	[5]	[5]	[5]	[5]	[5]
[6]	[6]	[6]	[6]	[6]	[6]	[6]
[7]	[7]	[7]	[7]	[7]	[7]	[7]
[8]	[8]	[8]	[8]	[8]	[8]	[8]
[9]	[9]	[9]	[9]	[9]	[9]	[9]

DATE OF BIRTH

Day		Month	Year
[0]	[0]	January	2011
[1]	[1]	February	2012
[2]	[2]	March	2013
[3]	[3]	April	2014
	[4]	May	2015
	[5]	June	2016
	[6]	July	2017
	[7]	August	2018
	[8]	September	2019
	[9]	October	2020
		November	2021
		December	2022

Roman Boy

1	2	3	4	5	6	7
A	A	A	A	A	A	A
B	B	B	B	B	B	B
C	C	C	C	C	C	C
D	D	D	D	D	D	D
E	E	E	E	E	E	E

8	9	10	11	12	13	14
A	A	A	A	A	A	A
B	B	B	B	B	B	B
C	C	C	C	C	C	C
D	D	D	D	D	D	D
E	E	E	E	E	E	E

15	16	17	18	19	20	21
A	A	A	A	A	A	A
B	B	B	B	B	B	B
C	C	C	C	C	C	C
D	D	D	D	D	D	D
E	E	E	E	E	E	E

22	23	24	25
A	A	A	A
B	B	B	B
C	C	C	C
D	D	D	D
E	E	E	E

Spelling

26	27	28	29	30	31	32	33
A	A	A	A	A	A	A	A
B	B	B	B	B	B	B	B
C	C	C	C	C	C	C	C
D	D	D	D	D	D	D	D
N	N	N	N	N	N	N	N

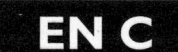

Punctuation: Football Fun

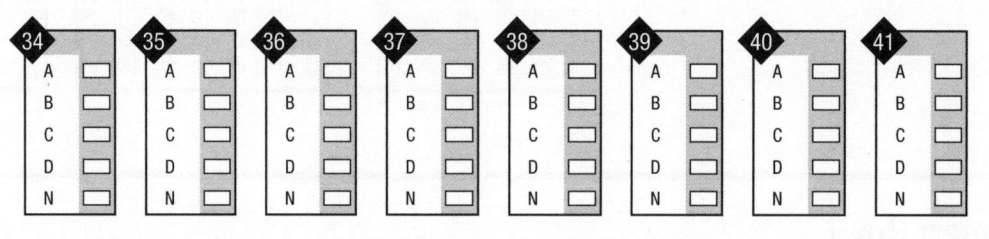

Word Selection: Ciaran the Conqueror

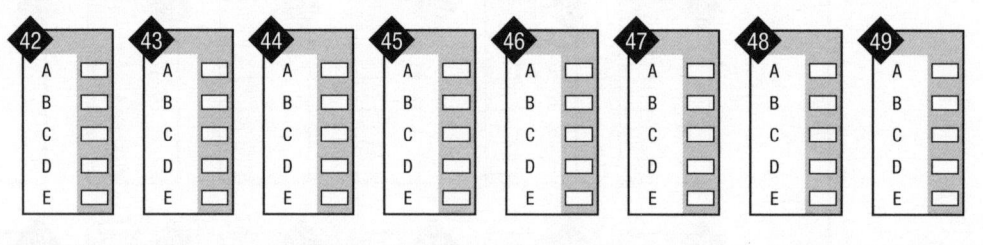

ENGLISH TEST D

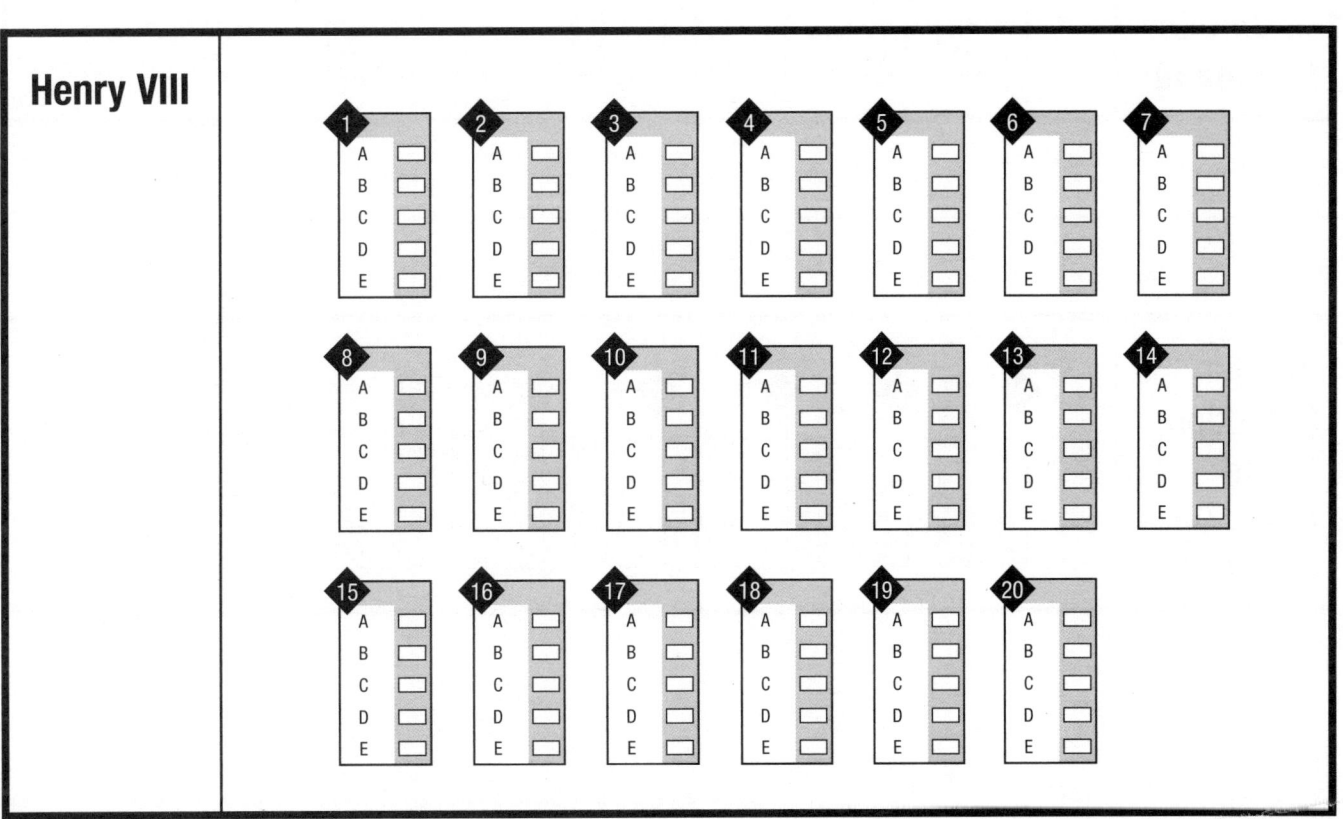

END

PUPIL NUMBER

Spelling: The Shooting of Archduke Ferdinand

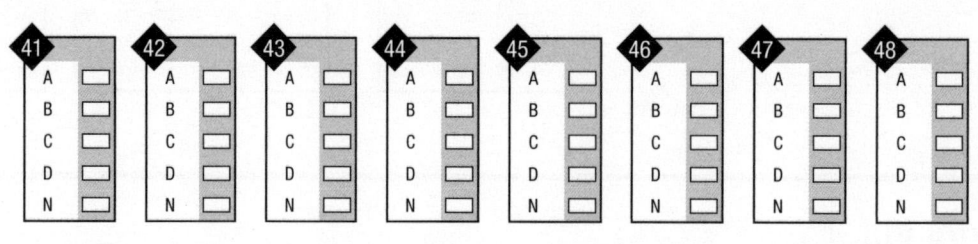

Word Selection: In the Deep, Dark Jungle

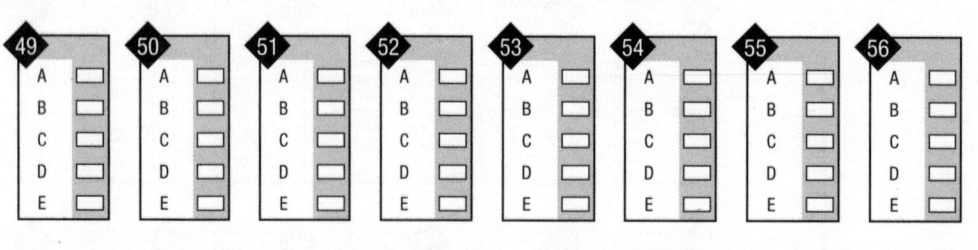